SOMATIC EXPERIENCING EXERCISES

for Healing Complex Trauma

HOPE ANDRUS

A Guide to Applying Grounding Exercises, Resourcing and Visualization, Self-Regulation, and Body Scan Techniques Alongside Your Therapy Journey

SOMATIC EXPERIENCING EXERCISES

for Healing Complex Trauma

A Guide to Applying Grounding Exercises, Resourcing and Visualization, Self-Regulation, and Body Scan Techniques Alongside Your Therapy Journey

HOPE ANDRUS

Editorial Director:
Lawrence Phillips
Cover Design:
Gabriel Glover
Editorial and Production Services:
True Pen Publishers

Preface

In the intricate tapestry of life, we often encounter experiences that leave deep scars. Complex trauma, in particular, can disrupt our sense of safety, security, and well-being. The body, as a wise and faithful guide, holds the key to unlocking the healing process.

This book, *Somatic Experiencing Exercises for Healing Complex Trauma*, invites you on a journey of self-discovery and healing. We will explore a variety of techniques designed to help you connect with your body, address the stored trauma responses, and cultivate a sense of peace and resilience.

Through grounding exercises, resourcing and visualization, self-regulation, and body scan techniques, you will learn to:

- **Anchor yourself in the present moment:** Grounding exercises, such as the 5-4-3-2-1 technique and body scan meditation, will help you stay present and reduce anxiety.

- **Tap into your inner strength:** Resourcing and visualization techniques, like creating a safe space and using positive affirmations, will empower you to draw on your resilience.

- **Manage stress and anxiety:** Self-regulation techniques, including relaxation exercises and emotional regulation strategies, will equip you to navigate difficult emotions.

- **Connect with your body on a deeper level:** Body scan techniques will allow you to release tension, promote healing, and cultivate a greater sense of self-awareness.

Remember, healing is a journey, not a destination. It's a process of rediscovering yourself, piece by piece. By embracing the techniques and strategies in this book, you can take significant steps toward healing and living a more fulfilling life.

The present moment is the only place where life exists. Grounding exercises help us to stay present and reduce anxiety by focusing our attention on our senses. By noticing the sights, sounds, smells, tastes, and sensations around us, we can anchor ourselves in the present moment and prevent our minds from wandering into the past or future.

Our minds are powerful tools that can be used to create positive change. Resourcing and visualization techniques help us to tap into our inner strength and resilience. By creating a safe space and using positive affirmations, we can fill our cups with hope, self-belief, and a sense of safety.

When we experience trauma, our nervous systems can become overactivated. Self-regulation techniques help us to calm our nervous systems and manage stress and anxiety. By practicing relaxation techniques and emotional regulation strategies, we can learn to respond to triggers in a healthy and adaptive way.

The body is a wise and faithful guide. Body scan techniques help us to connect with our bodies on a deeper level, releasing tension and promoting healing. By paying attention to our sensations and noticing areas of discomfort or tightness, we can identify and address the stored trauma responses in our bodies.

Healing from complex trauma is a process that requires patience, perseverance, and self-compassion. By embracing the techniques and strategies in this book, you can take significant steps toward healing and living a more fulfilling life. Remember, you are not alone on this journey. There are many people who care about you and want to support you. With time and effort, you can overcome the challenges of trauma and create a brighter future for yourself.

Contents

INTRODUCTION

Unlocking Your Body's Wisdom

"The body keeps the score." - Bessel van der Kolk

Somatic Experiencing (SE) is a transformative therapeutic approach designed to address trauma and stress-related disorders. Developed by Dr. Peter Levine, SE is grounded in the understanding that trauma is not solely a psychological issue but also a physiological one. This body-oriented therapy emphasizes the body's innate ability to heal itself, recognizing that traumatic experiences can disrupt the natural functioning of the autonomic nervous system. By focusing on the physical sensations associated with trauma, SE aims to help individuals process and release stored trauma responses, facilitating a return to a state of balance and well-being.

At its core, Somatic Experiencing operates on the principle that trauma often manifests as dysregulation within the body. When individuals experience trauma, their bodies may respond with a freeze response, akin to the fight-or-flight reaction. This response can lead to chronic tension and discomfort, as well as psychological symptoms like anxiety and depression. SE seeks to gently guide clients in developing an increased tolerance for difficult bodily sensations and emotions, allowing them to reconnect with their physical selves. This process begins by helping individuals become more aware of their internal bodily states—what practitioners refer to as interoception—thereby fostering a deeper understanding of how trauma has impacted their physical being.

In practice, SE involves a variety of techniques that promote bodily awareness and emotional regulation. During sessions, therapists encourage clients to notice their physical sensations without judgment, often employing methods such as "pendulation"—the rhythmic movement between states of arousal and calmness. This technique allows clients to gradually explore traumatic memories without becoming overwhelmed. Rather than reliving traumatic events in detail, SE focuses on the somatic experiences tied to those memories, enabling clients to "renegotiate" their relationship with trauma rather than simply rehashing it.

The effectiveness of Somatic Experiencing in healing complex trauma has been supported by various clinical studies and anecdotal evidence from practitioners and patients alike. For instance, randomized controlled trials have shown significant reductions in PTSD symptoms following SE treatment. Patients have reported not only decreased anxiety and depression but also improvements in physical symptoms such as chronic pain and sleep disturbances. Many individuals find that once they begin addressing the physical manifestations of their trauma through SE, they can more easily engage with the emotional aspects of their experiences.

In clinical settings, SE has been employed successfully across diverse populations, including survivors of abuse, veterans with combat-related PTSD, and individuals coping with grief or loss. Practitioners often highlight remarkable transformations in their clients' lives—stories of regained vitality, improved relationships, and enhanced emotional resilience are common. As clients learn to navigate their bodily sensations and release pent-up energy associated with trauma, they often experience a profound sense of liberation and empowerment.

Through Somatic Experiencing, individuals are not merely treated for their symptoms; they embark on a journey toward holistic healing that reconnects them with their bodies and restores their sense of safety in the world. This approach offers hope for those who have felt trapped by their past experiences, inviting them to reclaim their lives from the grip of unresolved trauma.

Addressing the body's stored trauma responses is crucial for holistic healing, as trauma can become deeply embedded within our physical and emotional systems. When individuals experience traumatic events, their bodies often react with intense physiological responses, such as increased heart rate, muscle tension, and the release of stress hormones like adrenaline. These reactions can lead to what is known as "trauma imprinting," where the body retains a memory of the trauma that manifests in various physical and emotional symptoms. For many, this results in chronic pain, anxiety, hypervigilance, and a host of other debilitating conditions that can persist long after the traumatic event has passed.

Trauma imprinting occurs at the moment of shock or fear during a traumatic experience. The brain records not only the event itself but also all sensory details associated with it—sounds, smells, sights, and even bodily sensations. This creates a lasting imprint in both the mind and body. For example, someone who has experienced a violent attack may find themselves feeling intense fear or physical discomfort upon encountering similar sensory stimuli in their environment, even if they are not consciously aware of why. This phenomenon illustrates how unprocessed trauma can manifest in the body's tissues and nervous system, leading to a cycle of distress that can be difficult to break.

Traditional talk therapy often falls short when it comes to addressing these physical manifestations of trauma. While it can be beneficial for exploring thoughts and feelings related to traumatic experiences, it typically does not engage with the body's stored responses. The rational part of the brain can become disconnected from the emotional centers during trauma, making it challenging for individuals to process their experiences through verbal communication alone. As a result, many people continue to live with unresolved trauma that affects their daily lives and overall well-being.

Scientific evidence supports the importance of addressing stored trauma responses through somatic approaches like Somatic Experiencing. Research has shown that unresolved trauma can lead to various health issues, including autoimmune disorders and chronic pain syndromes. A study highlighted that 50-70% of allergies could be traced back to traumatic experiences that needed to be cleared for proper immune function to resume.

Furthermore, trauma's effects can even extend transgenerationally; children of traumatized individuals may inherit not only psychological symptoms but also biological changes linked to their parents' experiences

Case studies further illustrate how addressing stored trauma responses can lead to profound healing. One case involved a woman who experienced chronic pain linked to childhood trauma. Through somatic techniques that focused on her autonomic nervous system (ANS), she was able to access memories associated with her pain and release the constriction held in her body. This process not only alleviated her physical symptoms but also allowed her to understand deeper emotional patterns that had been affecting her life.

The Mind-Body Connection in Trauma Recovery

The intricate relationship between the mind and body plays a pivotal role in trauma recovery, underscoring the necessity of addressing both aspects for effective healing. Trauma affects individuals not only psychologically but also physiologically, creating a complex interplay that can lead to a range of symptoms. When a person experiences trauma, their autonomic nervous system (ANS)—which regulates involuntary bodily functions—becomes activated, triggering responses that can lead to dysregulation. This dysregulation manifests as heightened states of arousal or, conversely, a shutdown response, both of which can have profound implications for mental and physical health.

The ANS consists of two main branches: the sympathetic nervous system (SNS), responsible for the "fight or flight" response, and the parasympathetic nervous system (PNS), which facilitates rest and relaxation. In moments of trauma, the SNS is activated, releasing stress hormones like cortisol and adrenaline. This response prepares the body to confront or flee from danger; however, when trauma is chronic or unresolved, the SNS can remain in a state of overdrive. This leads to symptoms such as anxiety, hypervigilance, and chronic pain, as the body struggles to return to its baseline state of calm. As noted by experts in the field, "When trauma is not resolved, the amygdala becomes chronically hyper-sensitized," making individuals more susceptible to stressors that would normally be interpreted as non-threatening by a well-functioning prefrontal cortex

1

.Understanding this mind-body connection is essential for developing effective treatment strategies. Traditional talk therapies often focus primarily on cognitive processes without adequately addressing the physiological responses embedded in the body. This oversight can leave significant gaps in recovery, as many individuals find that their emotional symptoms are intertwined with physical sensations and reactions. For example, someone might experience anxiety that is rooted not just in thoughts but also in tension held within their muscles or organs—a phenomenon that somatic experiencing seeks to address directly.

Somatic experiencing offers a pathway to re-establish balance within the ANS and promote overall well-being. By focusing on bodily sensations and encouraging clients to explore their physical experiences related to trauma, practitioners help individuals reconnect with their bodies in a safe and supportive environment. Techniques such as "pendulation," where clients oscillate between states of discomfort and comfort, allow them to gradually process traumatic memories without becoming overwhelmed. As Dr. Peter Levine explains, "The goal is not to relive the trauma but rather to renegotiate it," enabling clients to release stored energy associated with traumatic experiences. Case studies illustrate the effectiveness of somatic experiencing in facilitating this reconnection. One notable example involved a client who had experienced severe childhood trauma leading to chronic pain and anxiety. Through somatic techniques that engaged her

ANS, she was able to access memories that had been locked away in her body. As she processed these sensations and emotions, her physical symptoms began to diminish significantly. This experience highlights how addressing stored trauma responses can lead not only to emotional relief but also to tangible improvements in physical health.

The importance of recognizing and treating the mind-body connection in trauma recovery cannot be overstated. As noted by Bessel van der Kolk in his seminal work *The Body Keeps the Score*, "Trauma is not just an event that took place sometime in the past; it is also the imprint left by that experience on mind, brain, and body." This holistic understanding paves the way for more comprehensive treatment approaches that honor both psychological and physiological dimensions of healing. By integrating somatic practices into therapeutic frameworks, individuals can embark on a more complete journey toward recovery—one that embraces both their minds and bodies as integral parts of their healing process.

The Limitations of Traditional Talk Therapy for Trauma.

Traditional talk therapy has long been a cornerstone of mental health treatment, offering individuals a space to explore their thoughts and emotions. However, when it comes to addressing trauma, this approach often reveals significant limitations. While talk therapy can be incredibly valuable for many psychological issues, it primarily focuses on cognitive and emotional aspects, frequently neglecting the physical and physiological components that are equally crucial in the healing process. This oversight can lead to incomplete healing, allowing trauma symptoms to persist long after the initial event.

One of the primary challenges of traditional talk therapy in trauma recovery is its reliance on verbal communication. Traumatic memories are often difficult to access and articulate; the very nature of trauma can create barriers to effective communication. As noted by experts, "The very nature of traumatic memories makes them difficult to access, verbalize, and confront in a traditional talk therapy setting." This difficulty is compounded by the fact that trauma often leads to avoidance behaviors, where individuals may unconsciously steer clear of discussing painful experiences. Consequently, therapists who lack specialized training in trauma may inadvertently push clients to disclose more than they are ready for, which can lead to increased distress and further avoidance.

Moreover, research indicates that trauma can cause structural and functional changes in the brain. For instance, the amygdala—the brain's fear center—may become hyperactive in response to stress, while areas responsible for rational thought and decision-making, like the prefrontal cortex, may become less active. This imbalance complicates the therapeutic process; when clients are in a heightened state of arousal or distress, they may struggle to engage with cognitive therapies effectively. As Dr. Bessel van der Kolk states, "When the rational part of the brain is hijacked by the trauma memory, people may not hear words or reasoning or make meaning of events". This highlights a significant gap in traditional talk therapy: it often attempts to engage cognitive processes that may be offline during trauma responses.

Specific cases illustrate how traditional talk therapy has fallen short in effectively treating trauma. Consider Joe, a welder who suffered severe burns during an explosion. Despite his physical injuries being relatively minor, Joe experienced debilitating panic attacks and flashbacks that made returning to work impossible. In conventional therapy settings, he might have been encouraged to discuss his feelings about the event without addressing the underlying physiological responses his body was experiencing. This approach could leave him feeling more disconnected from his experience rather than facilitating healing.

To address these limitations, integrating somatic experiencing into therapeutic practices can provide a more holistic approach to trauma recovery. Somatic experiencing focuses on the body's sensations and responses rather than solely on thoughts and emotions. It emphasizes "bottom-up processing," which engages clients' physical experiences as a pathway toward healing. By helping individuals reconnect with their bodily sensations—such as tension or discomfort—therapists can guide them through the process of releasing stored trauma responses.

Research supports this integrative approach; studies have shown that somatic experiencing can lead to significant reductions in PTSD symptoms by addressing both emotional and physical aspects of trauma. For instance, clients who have engaged in somatic techniques often report not only emotional relief but also improvements in chronic pain and other physical symptoms tied to their traumatic experiences. The combination of cognitive understanding with somatic awareness allows individuals like Joe to process their trauma more fully, enabling them to reclaim their sense of safety and control.

The Role of Somatic Experiencing in Helping The Body Release Stored Trauma.

Somatic experiencing (SE) offers a unique and effective approach to releasing stored trauma from the body by focusing on the intricate interplay between physical sensations and emotional experiences. Developed by Dr. Peter Levine, SE recognizes that trauma is not merely a mental or emotional issue but also a deeply embodied one. By utilizing specific techniques, SE helps individuals gently navigate their bodily sensations, allowing for the release of pent-up trauma without overwhelming them.

One of the foundational techniques in somatic experiencing is **tracking bodily sensations**. This involves guiding clients to pay close attention to their internal physical experiences, such as tension, warmth, or discomfort. By encouraging individuals to observe these sensations without judgment, SE fosters a sense of safety and awareness that can be transformative. For instance, a client might notice a tightness in their chest when recalling a traumatic event. Rather than diving into the narrative of the trauma, the therapist encourages them to explore this sensation—what it feels like, where it resides in the body, and how it changes over time. This process helps individuals become more attuned to their bodies and promotes self-regulation.

Another key technique is **pendulation**, which refers to the oscillation between states of activation (where trauma responses may arise) and deactivation (a state of calm). This method allows clients to gradually experience discomfort associated with trauma while also learning to return to a state of relaxation. For example, during a session, a client might be guided to recall a distressing memory briefly—just enough to feel some activation—before shifting their focus back to a calming sensation or memory. This back-and-forth movement helps the nervous system recalibrate and reduces the overwhelming nature of traumatic memories. As Dr. Levine explains, "Pendulation allows us to safely explore our edges without being overwhelmed."

Titration is another essential technique in somatic experiencing that involves gradually increasing exposure to traumatic material in small doses. Instead of confronting a traumatic memory head-on, which can be re-traumatizing, titration allows clients to engage with their memories in manageable increments. For instance, if someone experienced significant loss, they might first explore feelings of sadness associated with that loss for just a few moments before returning to a more neutral or positive sensation. This approach not only helps prevent overwhelm but also enables clients to process their emotions at a pace that feels safe for them.

The effectiveness of these techniques is often illustrated through personal anecdotes and case studies. One such example involves Sarah, who had endured emotional abuse throughout her childhood. In traditional talk therapy, she found it challenging to articulate her feelings about her past experiences. However, through somatic experiencing, she began tracking her bodily sensations during sessions. As she focused on her tight shoulders and clenched jaw while recalling specific memories, she was able to release physical tension through breathwork and gentle movement. Over time, Sarah reported feeling lighter and more connected to her body, experiencing fewer anxiety attacks as she learned to navigate her sensations.

The role of a trained and experienced practitioner in facilitating this process cannot be overstated. A skilled SE therapist creates an environment of safety and trust, essential for clients to explore their bodies' sensations without fear of judgment or re-traumatization. They are adept at recognizing signs of distress and can guide clients back toward grounding techniques when necessary. As noted by experts in the field, "The therapeutic relationship is crucial; it provides the safety needed for clients to explore their trauma."

In summary, somatic experiencing offers powerful techniques like tracking bodily sensations, pendulation, and titration that effectively facilitate the release of stored trauma from the body. By focusing on the mind-body connection and ensuring safety through skilled guidance, individuals can embark on a healing journey that honors both their physical and emotional experiences.

Chapter 1

Grounding Exercises: Anchoring Yourself in the Present Moment

"The present moment is the only place where life exists." - Thich Nhat Hanh

"Breathing in, I calm my body. Breathing out, I smile. Dwelling in the present moment, I know this is a wonderful moment." This quote by Thich Nhat Hanh beautifully encapsulates the essence of mindfulness and living fully in the present. It serves as a gentle reminder that each moment we experience holds the potential for joy and peace if we choose to engage with it consciously. In a world filled with distractions and constant demands on our attention, grounding ourselves in the present moment becomes not just a practice but a necessity for our mental and emotional well-being.

The significance of this quote lies in its ability to ground us amidst the chaos of daily life. When we focus on our breath and acknowledge the present, we cultivate a sense of awareness that allows us to step back from our worries about the future or regrets about the past. This practice of mindfulness is transformative; it shifts our perspective from one of anxiety and distraction to one of clarity and appreciation. By embracing the present, we can savor simple pleasures—a warm cup of tea, a gentle breeze, or a smile from a loved one—finding beauty in what might otherwise feel mundane. This shift not only enhances our daily experiences but also fosters resilience against stress and emotional turmoil.

Being present is crucial for mental health because it helps us break free from cycles of negative thinking that can lead to anxiety and depression. When we dwell in the past or future, we often amplify feelings of regret or fear, which can cloud our judgment and hinder our ability to enjoy life. Grounding exercises, such as mindful breathing or walking meditation, allow us to reconnect with ourselves and our surroundings, promoting a sense of calm and stability. As we practice being present, we develop a deeper understanding of our thoughts and emotions, enabling us to respond rather than react to life's challenges.

This chapter will explore various techniques for cultivating mindfulness and grounding ourselves in the present moment. We will delve into practices such as mindful breathing, body scans, and sensory awareness exercises. Each technique offers unique benefits—from reducing stress and enhancing focus to improving emotional regulation and fostering self-compassion. By integrating these practices into our daily routines, we can create a more fulfilling life that honors the beauty of each moment.

As we embark on this journey together, remember that mindfulness is not about perfection; it's about progress. Each small step you take toward being present is a victory worth celebrating. Let's embrace this exploration with open hearts and minds, ready to discover the profound impact that living in the moment can have on our lives.

5-4-3-2-1 Technique

The 5-4-3-2-1 technique is a powerful grounding exercise that invites you to reconnect with the present moment by engaging your five senses. In times of stress or anxiety, this technique serves as a practical tool to anchor your mind and pull you away from overwhelming thoughts. By focusing on what you can see, touch, hear, smell, and taste, you create a sensory map that helps to stabilize your emotions and bring clarity to your experience.

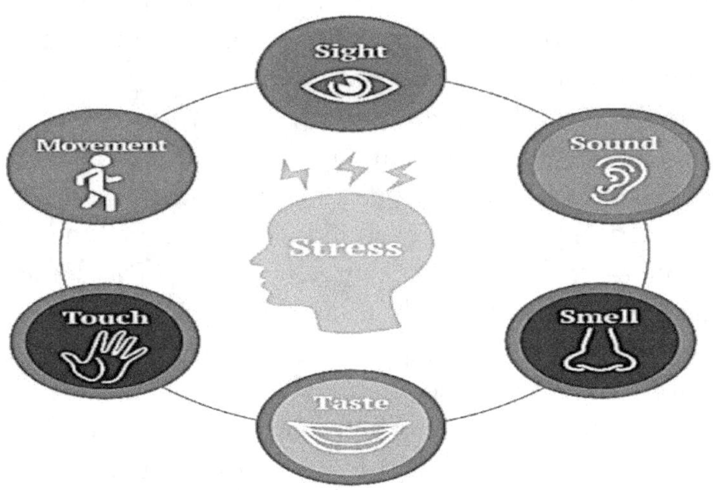

To begin, find a quiet space where you can sit comfortably. Take a deep breath in, feeling the air fill your lungs, and then exhale slowly, allowing any tension to melt away. Start with the first step: identify five things you can see around you. This could be anything from the color of the walls to the pattern on a rug or even a small object on your desk. As you name each item—"I see a blue book," "I see a window," "I see a plant"—allow yourself to really look at it. Notice its details, its texture, and how it fits into your environment. This act of observation pulls your attention away from anxious thoughts and into the richness of your surroundings.

Next, shift your focus to touch. Acknowledge four things you can physically feel. This might include the sensation of your feet on the ground, the fabric of your clothing against your skin, or even the warmth of sunlight streaming through a window. As you name each sensation—"I feel the coolness of the chair," "I feel my hair brushing against my neck"—take a moment to truly engage with these feelings. This tactile awareness reinforces your connection to the present moment and helps ground you in reality.

Then, turn your attention to sound. Listen carefully for three distinct noises in your environment. This could be the hum of an air conditioner, birds chirping outside, or even distant traffic sounds. As you identify each sound—"I hear the ticking clock," "I hear someone talking"—allow yourself to immerse in these auditory experiences. Each sound serves as an anchor that pulls you deeper into the now.

Afterward, focus on smell by identifying two scents around you. If you're in a familiar environment, perhaps you can catch the scent of freshly brewed coffee or a hint of cologne lingering in the air. If not, think of two favorite smells that evoke pleasant memories—like freshly baked cookies or blooming flowers—and visualize them vividly as you name them aloud. This olfactory engagement can evoke strong emotional responses and further connect you with positive feelings.

Finally, conclude with taste by identifying one flavor currently present in your mouth. It might be the lingering taste of toothpaste or perhaps something more recent like lunch or a snack. If nothing stands out, think about one of your favorite flavors—like chocolate or mint—and savor that thought for a moment. Engaging with this sense brings closure to the exercise while reinforcing your presence in the moment.

This technique is particularly useful during moments of high stress or anxiety because it shifts your focus from internal turmoil to external reality. By deliberately engaging each sense one at a time, you create a mental space where worries fade into the background and calmness takes precedence. The 5-4-3-2-1 technique not only helps alleviate immediate anxiety but also cultivates a habit of mindfulness that can enhance overall emotional resilience over time.

Examples of Specific Sights, Sounds, Smells, Tastes, and Sensations to Focus on.

Engaging with our senses is a delightful way to anchor ourselves in the present moment, and there are countless opportunities to do so in our everyday lives. When it comes to sights, take a moment to truly observe the patterns in a carpet beneath your feet. Notice how the colors intertwine, creating a tapestry of shapes that can draw you into a meditative state. If you're outside, allow yourself to be captivated by the vibrant colors of a flower, each petal telling its own story through hues of red, yellow, or blue. Or perhaps you find yourself gazing at the leaves dancing in the wind; watch how they flutter and sway, creating a gentle rhythm that mirrors the ebb and flow of life itself. Each visual experience invites you to slow down and appreciate the beauty that surrounds you.

The world of sound offers another rich tapestry for mindfulness. Take a moment to listen closely to the hum of your refrigerator; it's a steady background noise that often goes unnoticed but can serve as a comforting reminder of home. If you step outside, immerse yourself in the cheerful chirping of birds as they greet the morning or sing their evening lullabies. Their melodies can uplift your spirit and connect you with nature. And don't forget about the sound of your own breath; as you inhale and exhale, focus on the gentle rhythm it creates, a soothing reminder of your vitality and presence in this moment.

Smells have an incredible power to evoke memories and emotions, making them a wonderful avenue for mindfulness. Imagine brewing a fresh cup of coffee; as the aroma wafts through the air, take a moment to savor its rich scent before taking that first sip. Alternatively, lighting a scented candle can transform your space; allow yourself to be enveloped by its fragrance, whether it's soothing lavender or invigorating citrus. If you're outdoors after a rain shower, breathe deeply and enjoy the freshness of a rain-soaked garden; that earthy scent can be incredibly grounding and revitalizing.

When it comes to taste, there's so much joy in exploring flavors mindfully. Consider popping a piece of gum into your mouth; focus on its sweetness as it bursts forth and how it changes with every chew. Or perhaps you bite into a piece of fruit—notice the juiciness and sweetness that floods your senses with each bite. If you're feeling adventurous, indulge in dark chocolate; allow yourself to experience its rich bitterness slowly melting on your tongue, savoring every nuance of flavor.

Sensations remind us of our physical presence in the world around us. Feel your feet firmly planted on the ground; notice how this connection grounds you and provides stability. As you move through your day, pay attention to the texture of your clothing against your skin—perhaps it's soft cotton or cozy wool—and how it makes you feel comfortable or energized. When you hold a warm cup in your hands, take a moment to appreciate that warmth spreading through your palms and fingers; it's a simple pleasure that can bring comfort and joy.

As you explore these sensory experiences, remember that mindfulness is personal. Each person may find different elements resonate more deeply with them. So take your time—wander through your environment with curiosity and openness, discovering what delights your senses and brings you into the present moment. Embrace this journey of exploration; it's all about finding what works best for you and celebrating those moments of connection with yourself and the world around you.

Tips for Adapting This Technique to Different Situations.

The 5-4-3-2-1 technique is a wonderfully adaptable mindfulness exercise that can be tailored to fit various situations, helping you ground yourself and regain a sense of calm. Let's explore how you can modify this technique to suit different environments, whether you find yourself at work, in a bustling public place, or even grappling with a panic attack.

When at work, the office can sometimes feel overwhelming, filled with deadlines and distractions. To implement the 5-4-3-2-1 technique here, start by identifying five things you can see around you. This might be the patterns on your desk, the color of your colleagues' shirts, or the view outside your window. Next, focus on four things you can touch—perhaps the coolness of your keyboard, the texture of your chair, or even the warmth of your coffee cup. Then, listen for three distinct sounds; maybe it's the soft hum of the air conditioning, the chatter of coworkers, or the tapping of fingers on keyboards. For two smells, consider the scent of your lunch or the aroma of freshly brewed coffee wafting from the break room. Finally, take a moment to acknowledge one thing you can taste—maybe it's a lingering flavor from breakfast or simply the refreshing taste of water. This structured approach helps to redirect your focus and create a sense of stability amidst a busy workday.

In a public place, such as a crowded café or park, you might feel overwhelmed by the noise and activity around you. Here, you can still engage with the 5-4-3-2-1 technique by using your surroundings creatively. Start by observing five things you can see; perhaps it's people walking by, colorful decorations on walls, or even animals playing nearby. If physical items are limited or hard to identify due to movement, you can use mental imagery instead—visualize five different colors or shapes that represent calmness to you. Next, focus on four things you can touch; this could be the fabric of your clothing or the coolness of a metal bench. If external stimuli are limited, turn inward and concentrate on internal sensations—like how your heart feels as it beats steadily in your chest. For sounds in this lively environment, listen for three distinct noises; maybe it's laughter from nearby tables, music playing softly in the background, or even the rustling of leaves in the wind. When it comes to smells, think about two aromas that bring comfort—perhaps imagining fresh bread baking or flowers blooming nearby. Finally, acknowledge one taste; if you have a drink with you, savor its flavor consciously or recall a favorite food that brings you joy.

During moments of heightened anxiety or panic attacks, adapting this technique becomes even more crucial. In such instances where external stimuli may feel overwhelming or inaccessible, focusing on internal sensations can provide significant relief. Start with five internal sensations—notice how your feet feel against the ground or how your chest rises and falls with each breath. You might also focus on how tension feels in different areas of your body; perhaps there's tightness in your shoulders or warmth in your hands. Move on to four emotions that arise; acknowledge feelings like anxiety, fear, calmness, or hope without judgment. Then identify three thoughts that come to mind; they could be worries about the future or reminders of past successes that ground you in reality. For two affirmations that resonate with you—like "I am safe" or "This feeling will pass"— repeat them gently to yourself as mantras. Lastly, focus on one positive memory that brings comfort; perhaps it's a cherished moment spent with loved ones or an accomplishment that fills you with pride.

The beauty of the 5-4-3-2-1 technique lies in its flexibility and adaptability across various contexts. Whether you're at work navigating deadlines and distractions or out in public surrounded by noise and movement—or even facing moments of anxiety—it remains a powerful tool for grounding yourself and fostering mindfulness. Embrace this versatility and allow yourself to explore what resonates most with you in each unique situation; it's all about finding what brings you back to center and helps cultivate peace within yourself.

Body Scan Meditation

Body scan meditation is a beautiful way to cultivate awareness of your body and release any tension you may be holding. It invites you to connect deeply with yourself, fostering relaxation and mindfulness. Let's walk through a step-by-step guide to help you embark on this calming journey.

Begin by finding a comfortable position, either lying down on your back or sitting in a chair with your feet flat on the ground. If you choose to lie down, let your arms rest gently at your sides or place them on your belly. If you're sitting, keep your back straight but relaxed, allowing your shoulders to drop away from your ears. Once you've settled into your position, gently close your eyes. This simple action can help minimize distractions and create a sense of inner focus.

Now, take a deep breath in through your nose, allowing your belly to rise as you fill your lungs with air. Hold that breath for just a moment, and then exhale slowly through your mouth, letting go of any tension or stress you may be carrying. Repeat this deep breathing two more times—inhale deeply, hold it for a moment, and then exhale fully. With each breath, feel yourself becoming more grounded and present in this moment.

As you settle into this space, bring your attention to your toes. Notice any sensations—perhaps warmth, tingling, or even tightness. If you feel any discomfort or tension, imagine breathing into that area. Inhale deeply, envisioning the breath flowing into your toes, and as you exhale, visualize that tension melting away like ice under the sun. Spend a moment here before gently moving your awareness up to the soles of your feet. Acknowledge how they feel against the surface beneath you.

Next, shift your focus to the tops of your feet and ankles. Notice any sensations present—are they relaxed or tense? Again, breathe into any areas of tightness or discomfort. Allow each exhale to carry away any lingering tension as you continue this process up through the arches of your feet and into your heels.

Now guide your attention to your calves. Observe how they feel; are they heavy or light? Are there areas that feel particularly tight? Breathe into those sensations and allow yourself to release any discomfort with each exhale. Move up to your knees and thighs, noticing how they connect with the ground or chair. Take a moment here to appreciate the strength of these muscles that support you.

Continuing upward, bring awareness to your hips and pelvis. This area often holds stress and tension; as you breathe deeply, visualize sending warmth and relaxation into these muscles. Allow any tightness to dissipate as you exhale.

Now focus on your lower back and abdomen. Notice how they feel as you breathe; does the breath rise and fall in these areas? If there's discomfort or tension, breathe into it gently, allowing each exhale to release that tightness.Shift your attention now to your upper back and shoulders. These areas can often carry significant stress from daily life. As you breathe in deeply, imagine filling this space with warmth and light; as you exhale, let go of any burdens you may be holding onto.

Bring awareness to your neck now; notice how it feels as it supports your head. If there's any tension here—perhaps from looking at screens or holding stress—breathe into it fully. With each exhale, allow that tension to flow out of your body.

Now focus on your jaw and facial muscles. Notice if you're clenching or holding tension in these areas; if so, take a deep breath in and consciously relax these muscles as you exhale. Allow the sensation of relaxation to wash over your face—softening the forehead, relaxing the eyes, and releasing any tightness around the mouth.

Finally, bring awareness to the crown of your head. Feel the connection between this area and the rest of your body; take a moment to appreciate how every part is interconnected. As you breathe in one last time, visualize drawing in peace and calmness from above; as you exhale, let go of anything that no longer serves you.

As you conclude this body scan meditation, take a few moments to simply breathe deeply again—inhale peace and calmness while exhaling tension and stress. When you're ready, gently wiggle your fingers and toes before slowly opening your eyes.

Feel free to use key phrases during this meditation for added support: "I breathe in relaxation," "I release tension," "I am present in my body," or "I honor my feelings." These affirmations can deepen the experience and enhance self-awareness throughout the practice.

Remember that body scan meditation is a personal journey; it's perfectly okay if certain sensations arise or if some areas feel more tense than others. The goal is not to change anything but simply to observe with kindness and curiosity. Embrace this practice as an opportunity for self-care and connection with yourself!

BENEFITS OF BODY SCAN MEDITATION FOR GROUNDING AND RELAXATION.

Body scan meditation is a powerful practice that offers a myriad of benefits, making it a valuable addition to anyone's self-care routine. One of the most immediate advantages is its ability to **reduce stress**. In our fast-paced lives, we often find ourselves caught up in a whirlwind of thoughts and responsibilities, which can lead to feelings of overwhelm. By focusing on different parts of the body, body scan meditation helps redirect our attention from the chaos of daily life to the simple sensations within us. This shift creates a calming effect, allowing us to unwind and release built-up tension.

Another significant benefit of this practice is the enhancement of **body awareness**. Many of us move through life disconnected from our physical selves, often ignoring signals our bodies send us about discomfort or stress. Body scan meditation encourages you to tune in and listen to your body, fostering a deeper understanding of where you may be holding tension or experiencing discomfort. This heightened awareness can lead to more mindful choices in daily activities, such as how we sit at our desks or how we carry stress in our shoulders.

The practice also promotes **enhanced relaxation**. As you systematically focus on each part of your body, you create an opportunity to consciously release tension. Breathing into areas that feel tight and allowing them to soften can lead to profound relaxation. This not only feels good in the moment but can also help improve your overall quality of sleep. Many practitioners report that regular body scan meditation leads to better sleep patterns, as the practice encourages a state of calm that can carry over into the evening.

On a psychological level, body scan meditation has been shown to significantly reduce **anxiety**. By grounding yourself in the present moment and focusing on physical sensations rather than spiraling thoughts about the past or future, you can break the cycle of anxious thinking. This mindfulness practice activates the parasympathetic nervous system—the part responsible for rest and digestion—helping to calm your mind and body during stressful moments.

Physiologically, engaging in body scan meditation can lead to improved **overall well-being**. Research indicates that mindfulness practices like this can lower blood pressure, reduce chronic pain, and even enhance immune function. By fostering a mind-body connection, you not only become more aware of how stress affects your body but also learn techniques to manage it effectively.

Grounding is another key aspect of body scan meditation. By bringing attention back to your physical body and anchoring yourself in the present moment, you cultivate a sense of stability and security. This grounding effect is particularly beneficial when life feels chaotic or overwhelming; it serves as a reminder that you are here, in this moment, fully supported by your surroundings.

Incorporating body scan meditation into your routine can be transformative. It's not just about achieving relaxation or reducing anxiety; it's about building a deeper connection with yourself and fostering an ongoing awareness of your feelings and sensations. Each time you practice, you're not only taking steps toward immediate relief but also nurturing long-term health benefits that contribute to your overall well-being. As you explore this technique, remember that it's about the journey— embracing each moment as it comes and allowing yourself the grace to simply be.

Tips for Dealing with Uncomfortable Sensations During Body Scan

Experiencing uncomfortable sensations during a body scan can be challenging, but it's an essential part of the mindfulness journey. Here are some practical strategies to help you handle these sensations with grace and compassion.

Embrace a Non-Judgmental Attitude

First and foremost, it's crucial to approach any discomfort with a non-judgmental mindset. Instead of labeling sensations as "good" or "bad," try to simply acknowledge them as part of your experience. This shift in perspective can be incredibly liberating.

- **Practice Awareness**: When discomfort arises, take a moment to notice it without reacting. Simply observe the sensation as if you were watching clouds pass by in the sky—there, but not permanent.

Acknowledge Without Reacting

When you feel discomfort, acknowledge its presence without the urge to change it immediately. This acknowledgment can create space for acceptance.

- **Name the Sensation**: Silently name what you're feeling—"tightness," "pressure," or "tingling." This simple act can help you detach from the sensation and reduce its intensity.

Visualization Techniques

Visualizing can be a powerful tool for managing discomfort during your practice. Here are a couple of techniques to try:

- **Dissolving Visualization**: Imagine the uncomfortable sensation as a solid object—perhaps a rock or a knot. Visualize it slowly dissolving into warm light or melting away like ice in the sun. This imagery can help soften the sensation and make it feel less daunting.
- **Breathing Light**: As you breathe in, visualize drawing in soothing light that fills your body. On your exhale, imagine releasing any discomfort or tension. This technique not only helps manage sensations but also promotes relaxation.

Use Affirmations

Positive affirmations can be incredibly supportive during moments of discomfort. They serve as gentle reminders that you are safe and capable of handling whatever arises.

- **Simple Affirmations**: Try repeating phrases like "I am safe," "This too shall pass," or "I welcome this sensation with compassion." You can say these silently in your mind or out loud if that feels comfortable.

Cultivating Self-Compassion

Self-compassion is key when navigating uncomfortable sensations. Remember that it's perfectly normal to experience discomfort during mindfulness practices; you are not alone in this journey.

- **Be Gentle with Yourself**: If you find yourself feeling frustrated or overwhelmed, take a moment to acknowledge that this is part of being human. Treat yourself with the same kindness you would offer a friend in a similar situation.

Practice Patience

Lastly, patience is essential in this practice. Just as sensations come and go, so too will your feelings about them.

- **Allow Time**: Give yourself permission to sit with discomfort for a few moments longer than you might usually choose to. Often, simply allowing space for the sensation can lead to its natural ebbing away.

By integrating these strategies into your body scan practice, you'll cultivate a more supportive and nurturing environment for yourself. Remember, every experience is an opportunity for growth and understanding.

Deep Breathing Exercises

Deep breathing is more than just a simple act of inhaling and exhaling; it's a powerful physiological tool that can significantly impact our nervous system and overall well-being. When we engage in deep breathing, especially techniques like diaphragmatic breathing, we activate the parasympathetic nervous system, which is often referred to as the "rest and digest" system. This activation is crucial because it counters the sympathetic nervous system, responsible for our fight-or-flight response. By focusing on deep, controlled breaths, we can shift our body from a state of stress and anxiety to one of calm and relaxation.

As we take deeper breaths, we stimulate the vagus nerve, which plays a vital role in regulating heart rate and promoting relaxation. This stimulation leads to a decrease in heart rate and a lowering of blood pressure. Research has shown that regular practice of deep breathing can lead to significant reductions in both systolic and diastolic blood pressure. For instance, a meta-analysis encompassing numerous studies indicated that deep breathing exercises could lower systolic blood pressure by an average of 6 mmHg and diastolic pressure by 3 to 6 mmHg over time, comparable to other nonpharmacological interventions like dietary changes or aerobic exercise. Moreover, deep breathing helps reduce the levels of cortisol, the body's primary stress hormone. Elevated cortisol levels are linked to various health issues, including anxiety, depression, and cardiovascular disease. By consciously engaging in deep breathing exercises, we can effectively lower cortisol levels and mitigate these negative effects. Studies have demonstrated that individuals who practice deep breathing regularly report lower feelings of anxiety and stress.

In practical terms, techniques such as the "4-7-8" breathing method exemplify how structured breathing patterns can enhance relaxation. In this technique, one inhales for four counts, holds the breath for seven counts, and exhales slowly for eight counts. This rhythmic pattern not only encourages mindfulness but also promotes physiological changes that support relaxation. The act of focusing on breath control diverts attention from stressors and fosters a sense of tranquility.

The benefits extend beyond just immediate relaxation; they can also improve long-term mental health. Chronic stress often leads to heightened anxiety or depressive symptoms, but consistent practice of deep breathing has been shown to alleviate these conditions over time. For example, a study found that participants who engaged in regular deep breathing exercises experienced significant reductions in anxiety levels after just a few weeks

.In addition to these mental health benefits, deep breathing enhances oxygen delivery throughout the body. When we breathe deeply, we engage our diaphragm more effectively, allowing for greater lung capacity and improved oxygen exchange. This increased oxygen supply not only fuels our organs but also supports optimal brain function and energy levels

Mindfulness of Movement

By engaging fully with the present moment, we can break free from the mindless, automatic behaviors that often dominate our routines. This practice invites us to become aware of the subtleties of our physical experience, fostering a deeper connection between body and mind.

Imagine standing at the bathroom sink, toothbrush in hand. Instead of rushing through this mundane task, take a moment to notice how your feet feel against the floor. Are they firmly grounded, or do they shift slightly as you move? As you begin to brush your teeth, pay attention to the sensation of the bristles against your gums and teeth. Notice the rhythm of your breath as you work—perhaps it becomes slower and more deliberate, or maybe it quickens with excitement as you engage in this simple act. This awareness transforms brushing your teeth from a chore into a mindful ritual, enhancing your presence in the moment.

Washing dishes offers another opportunity for mindfulness. As you stand at the sink, feel the warmth of the water as it flows over your hands. Notice the weight of each dish as you scrub away remnants of meals past. Pay attention to the sounds—the clinking of plates, the splash of water—as they create a symphony of domestic life. Each movement can be an invitation to breathe deeply and center yourself in the here and now. Let your mind drift away from distractions and focus solely on this act of cleansing, allowing it to ground you in the present.

Walking to the mailbox can also become a mindful practice. Instead of letting your mind wander to tasks awaiting you or thoughts about the day ahead, bring your attention to each step you take. Feel the ground beneath your feet—the texture of the pavement or grass—and notice how your legs propel you forward. Observe how your arms swing gently at your sides, perhaps feeling a slight breeze against your skin. As you breathe in and out, notice how each breath aligns with your movements, creating a harmonious rhythm that connects you deeply with your surroundings.

In these moments—whether brushing teeth, washing dishes, or walking—encourage yourself to notice not just what you're doing but how it feels. What sensations arise? Is there tension in your shoulders as you scrub a stubborn pot? Do you feel a sense of lightness in your step as you walk? By tuning into these physical experiences, you cultivate a sense of presence that enriches even the simplest activities.

Examples of Mindful Movement Activities, Such as Walking, Yoga, or Gardening.

Mindfulness can be seamlessly integrated into various activities, transforming ordinary moments into profound experiences of presence and awareness. One such activity is walking, which offers a beautiful opportunity to connect with the environment and oneself. As you walk, begin by bringing your attention fully to the sensation of each step. Feel the weight of your foot as it lifts off the ground, the moment it hovers in the air, and the gentle impact as it meets the earth again. Notice the texture of the ground beneath you—whether it's the soft give of grass, the coolness of pavement, or the crunch of gravel. Allow your breath to synchronize with your movement; inhale deeply as you step forward, and exhale fully as your foot touches down. This rhythmic connection between breath and movement not only grounds you in the present moment but also cultivates a sense of calm and clarity.

Yoga is another powerful practice that invites mindfulness into our daily lives. As you transition through various poses, focus on the alignment of your body. Pay attention to how each part interacts with the others; notice how your spine lengthens in downward dog or how your hips open in warrior pose. Feel the flow of your breath as it guides your movements—inhale to expand, exhale to release tension. This conscious breathing enhances your awareness of sensations in your muscles, allowing you to tune into areas that may hold stress or tightness. By fostering this deep connection between breath and body, yoga becomes not just a physical practice but a meditative journey that promotes relaxation and mental clarity.

Gardening also serves as a rich arena for mindfulness, encouraging a deep engagement with nature. As you dig your hands into the soil, pay close attention to its texture—the coolness against your skin, the grains slipping through your fingers. Notice the earthy aroma that rises as you turn over the dirt, a scent that is both grounding and invigorating. As you tend to plants, observe their colors and shapes; take in the delicate fragrances they emit and how they change throughout the day. Feel the rhythm of your movements as you plant seeds or prune branches; each action becomes an expression of care and intention. This sensory immersion fosters a profound sense of peace and connection to nature, reducing stress and enhancing overall well-being.

Engaging mindfully in these activities not only helps ground us but also cultivates resilience against life's stresses. By focusing on our breath, body sensations, and surroundings, we create a sanctuary within ourselves where we can find solace amid chaos. Each mindful moment serves as a reminder that peace is always accessible if we choose to embrace it through our everyday actions.

The Benefits of Mindfulness of Movement for Grounding and Stress Reduction.

Mindfulness of movement is a transformative practice that intertwines physical activity with a heightened sense of awareness, offering a multitude of benefits for both mental and emotional well-being. At its core, this approach encourages individuals to engage with their bodies in a way that fosters improved body awareness. As people move mindfully, they begin to notice the subtleties of their physical sensations and movements, which can lead to a deeper understanding of how their bodies feel in different states. This increased awareness can illuminate patterns of tension or discomfort, allowing individuals to address these issues proactively rather than reactively. Research has shown that participants in mindful movement programs often report significant reductions in negative emotions, with one study indicating up to a 33% decrease in stress levels after just eight weeks of practice.

The act of moving mindfully also serves as a powerful antidote to stress. In our fast-paced lives, where the mind often races ahead or lingers on past worries, mindful movement invites us to anchor ourselves in the present moment. By focusing on the rhythm of our breath and the sensations in our bodies, we can create a mental space that allows for relaxation and release from accumulated tension. Moving meditation practices, such as walking or gentle stretching, shift attention away from daily anxieties and immerse us in the experience of being alive right now. This redirection not only calms the mind but also promotes emotional health by enhancing our ability to respond to feelings rather than react impulsively.

Moreover, mindfulness of movement is particularly beneficial for managing anxiety. For many individuals who struggle with anxious thoughts, traditional seated meditation can feel daunting or even counterproductive. Mindful movement provides an alternative pathway to mindfulness that is more accessible for those who find it difficult to sit still. Engaging in activities like tai chi or yoga allows practitioners to focus on their movements and breathing while simultaneously cultivating a sense of calm. This practice encourages staying present rather than getting lost in spirals of worry about the future or ruminations about the past.

Personal anecdotes abound regarding the calming effects of mindful movement. Many individuals have shared how incorporating mindful walking into their daily routine has helped them navigate stressful situations more gracefully. For instance, one person described taking deliberate steps during a particularly challenging day at work; as they focused on each footfall and their breath, they found themselves feeling more grounded and less overwhelmed by external pressures. Such experiences highlight how mindful movement can serve as both a coping mechanism and a preventive strategy against anxiety.

Scientific evidence further supports these observations. Studies indicate that mindful movement practices not only reduce stress but also enhance overall emotional resilience. Participants who engaged in regular mindful movement reported not only lower levels of anxiety but also improved mood and greater life satisfaction over time. The integration of body awareness with mindfulness creates a unique synergy that empowers individuals to manage their emotions more effectively.

In essence, mindfulness of movement fosters an enriched connection to the present moment while simultaneously promoting a sense of calm and clarity amidst life's chaos. By embracing this practice, individuals can cultivate an inner sanctuary—one where stress diminishes, body awareness flourishes, and emotional well-being becomes more attainable..

Nature Connection

Spending time in nature has long been recognized as a powerful antidote to the stresses of modern life. The concept of "forest bathing," or *Shinrin-yoku*, originated in Japan during the 1980s as a response to rising health concerns linked to urbanization and technology. This practice encourages individuals to immerse themselves in the forest environment, engaging all five senses to foster a deep connection with nature. Unlike traditional hiking, which often prioritizes physical exertion, forest bathing emphasizes mindfulness and presence, allowing participants to experience the calming effects of the natural world.The benefits of forest bathing are both profound and varied. Research has demonstrated that simply being in a forest can significantly reduce levels of cortisol, the body's primary stress hormone. One study found that participants who engaged in forest bathing experienced a reduction in cortisol levels by as much as 12.4 percent compared to those who walked in urban settings. This reduction in stress not only enhances emotional well-being but also contributes to improved physical health. Lower cortisol levels are associated with decreased risks of chronic illnesses such as hypertension and heart disease, highlighting how nature acts as a buffer against the pressures of daily life.Beyond stress reduction, forest bathing has been linked to improved mood and emotional resilience. The tranquil environment of the forest helps individuals shift their focus from anxieties and worries to the sensory experiences around them—the rustling leaves, the scent of pine needles, and the dappled sunlight filtering through the trees. This sensory immersion fosters a state of mindfulness that can alleviate symptoms of anxiety and depression. Studies indicate that participants report feeling more relaxed, happy, and connected after spending time among the trees, with some experiencing up to a 50% increase in creative problem-solving abilities following just a few days of forest exposure.

Moreover, the physical health benefits of forest bathing extend beyond mental well-being. The trees release phytoncides—natural essential oils that have antimicrobial properties—which can enhance immune function. Research has shown that spending time in forests increases the activity of natural killer cells, which play a crucial role in combating viruses and cancer cells. This immune boost can last for weeks after a single visit to a forested area, illustrating how nature not only nurtures our minds but also fortifies our bodies.

The restorative effects of nature are further amplified by its ability to improve attention and cognitive function. In our fast-paced world filled with digital distractions, stepping into a forest provides an opportunity for mental rejuvenation. Engaging with nature allows our minds to reset, reducing mental fatigue and enhancing focus. This phenomenon is akin to a form of natural therapy that invites us to slow down and reconnect with our surroundings.

Forest bathing is more than just a leisurely stroll; it is an invitation to cultivate a deeper relationship with nature and ourselves. As we navigate through life's complexities, taking time to immerse ourselves in the natural world can serve as a vital practice for maintaining balance and well-being. Whether it's through guided sessions led by trained therapists or simply finding solace in a nearby park, embracing the healing power of nature offers an accessible pathway toward improved mental and emotional health.

Connecting with Nature

Connecting with nature is one of the most enriching experiences we can have, and there are countless ways to immerse ourselves in the beauty and tranquility that the natural world offers. Imagine stepping into a nearby park, where the sun filters through the leaves, casting playful shadows on the ground. As you stroll along the winding paths, take a moment to pause and truly absorb your surroundings. Listen closely to the gentle rustling of leaves in the breeze, the cheerful chirping of birds flitting from branch to branch, and the distant laughter of children playing. Each sound is a reminder of life thriving all around you, inviting you to be a part of it.

Finding a serene spot by a body of water can be another delightful way to connect with nature. Whether it's a tranquil lake, a babbling brook, or even the ocean's rhythmic waves, sitting by water has a calming effect that can soothe even the busiest minds. As you settle down on a soft patch of grass or a smooth rock, close your eyes for a moment and focus on the sounds of water lapping at the shore or flowing over stones. Feel the cool breeze against your skin and inhale deeply, allowing the fresh scent of wet earth and aquatic plants to fill your lungs. You might even notice tiny ripples dancing across the surface, reflecting sunlight like diamonds scattered across a blue canvas.

Gardening offers another profound connection to nature, allowing you to engage with it on a personal level. Whether you have a sprawling backyard or just a few pots on your balcony, tending to plants can be incredibly rewarding. Digging your hands into rich soil connects you physically to the earth, while nurturing seeds into blooming flowers or fresh vegetables fosters a sense of responsibility and accomplishment. As you work, pay attention to the textures around you—the roughness of bark, the softness of petals, and even the gritty feel of soil slipping through your fingers. The fragrances released by herbs like basil or mint can transport you to another place entirely, evoking memories and sparking joy.

Bird watching is another captivating way to engage with nature that invites patience and observation. Grab a comfortable chair or blanket and find a quiet spot where feathered friends are likely to visit—perhaps near trees or feeders in your yard. Bring along binoculars if you have them and take note of their colors, sizes, and behaviors. You might witness an industrious woodpecker hammering away at a tree trunk or a graceful hawk gliding overhead. Allow yourself to be fully present in these moments; listen for their calls and songs, which can range from melodious tunes to sharp chirps. Each sighting becomes an exciting treasure hunt as you learn about different species and their unique habits.

Another delightful activity is collecting leaves during autumn when they transform into vibrant hues of red, orange, and yellow. Take a leisurely walk through your neighborhood or local park with an eye for interesting shapes and colors. As you gather leaves, consider their textures—some may be smooth while others are crinkly or velvety. When you return home, spread them out on a table and admire their beauty; perhaps even press them between pages of a heavy book for future crafting projects. This simple act not only connects you with nature but also ignites creativity as you think about how these natural treasures can be incorporated into art or decoration.

Simply sitting under a tree can be one of life's most peaceful pleasures. Find your favorite tree—perhaps one with sprawling branches that provide ample shade—and make yourself comfortable at its base. Lean back against its sturdy trunk and let your mind wander as you gaze up at the canopy above. Notice how sunlight filters through the leaves in dappled patterns on your skin while listening to the whispers of branches swaying gently in the wind.

This moment allows for reflection and mindfulness; it's an opportunity to disconnect from technology and reconnect with yourself amidst nature's embrace.

The Benefits of Nature Connection for Grounding and Reducing Anxiety

Connecting with nature offers a multitude of benefits that can significantly enhance our mental and emotional well-being. The simple act of stepping outside, feeling the earth beneath our feet, and immersing ourselves in the natural world can lead to reduced anxiety, improved mood, and a profound sense of overall well-being. Scientific research has shown that spending time in nature can lower cortisol levels, the hormone associated with stress, which in turn helps alleviate feelings of anxiety and tension. For instance, studies indicate that grounding—walking barefoot on natural surfaces—can lead to measurable improvements in stress levels and emotional health by fostering a deeper connection with the earth's energy.

The grounding effect of nature is not merely anecdotal; it is supported by various scientific findings. When we engage with the earth directly, whether through walking on grass or sitting under a tree, we tap into its natural electric charge. This interaction has been linked to numerous health benefits, including reduced inflammation and improved sleep quality. The physical sensations experienced during these moments—like the coolness of grass or the warmth of sunlight—help anchor us in the present, allowing us to escape the relentless pace of modern life. This sensory engagement can shift our focus from overwhelming thoughts to tangible experiences, providing a calming effect that enhances our mood and promotes relaxation.

Moreover, being in nature fosters a sense of stability and connection to something larger than ourselves. This grounding experience can evoke feelings of belonging and peace, as if we are part of a greater whole. Many people report that spending time outdoors helps them feel more centered and connected to their surroundings. For example, leaning against a tree or simply observing the intricate details of a flower can create a sense of balance and harmony within ourselves. This connection is essential in today's fast-paced world where technology often isolates us from our natural environment.

Personal anecdotes further illustrate these benefits. Many individuals share stories of how a walk in the woods or a day at the beach transformed their mood from anxious or overwhelmed to calm and rejuvenated. These moments spent in nature allow for reflection and mindfulness, encouraging us to appreciate the beauty around us while also giving our minds a much-needed break from constant stimulation. Incorporating regular nature connections into our daily lives can be transformative. Whether it's taking a short walk during lunch breaks, practicing yoga outdoors, or simply enjoying a moment of stillness in a park, these small acts can lead to significant improvements in mental health and emotional resilience. By prioritizing time spent in nature, we not only enhance our well-being but also cultivate a deeper appreciation for the world around us.

Chapter 2

Resourcing and Visualization: Filling Your Cup

"Imagination is everything. It is the preview of life's coming attractions." - Albert Einstein

Creating a Safe Space

Creating a dedicated safe space for visualization can profoundly impact psychological and emotional well-being. This sanctuary, whether a physical location or an imagined environment, serves as a refuge from the chaos of daily life, offering a place where individuals can unwind and reconnect with themselves. The essence of a safe space lies in its ability to foster feelings of emotional and physical security, which are essential for effective visualization practices. When individuals feel safe, they are more likely to engage deeply in their visualization exercises, allowing their minds to explore and create without the interference of anxiety or self-doubt.

The benefits of having a safe space extend beyond mere relaxation; they significantly enhance focus and concentration. In a world filled with distractions, having a designated area that is free from interruptions allows for a more profound commitment to the practice of visualization. This focused environment encourages individuals to immerse themselves in their thoughts and intentions, making it easier to visualize goals and aspirations clearly. The act of creating boundaries around this space—whether by setting aside specific times for use or ensuring it remains free from technology—reinforces its purpose as a haven for mental clarity and creativity.

Moreover, the psychological impact of a safe space is particularly beneficial in reducing anxiety. For many, anxiety can stem from feeling overwhelmed by external pressures or internal conflicts. A safe space acts as an antidote to this stress by providing an environment where one can feel completely at ease. Engaging in visualization within such a context allows individuals to process their emotions and thoughts without judgment or fear. This sense of safety can lead to deeper relaxation, enabling the body to release tension and the mind to quieten. Activities like meditation or deep breathing can be seamlessly integrated into this space, further enhancing the calming effects.

The role of a safe space in promoting comfort cannot be understated. It becomes a personal sanctuary that individuals can return to whenever they need solace or inspiration. This consistent access to a comforting environment helps cultivate a sense of belonging and stability, essential components for emotional health. When individuals know they have a place where they can express themselves freely and without fear, it nurtures self-acceptance and encourages personal growth.

In addition to these benefits, the practice of visualization itself can be enriched within a safe space. Visualization often requires one to tap into their imagination fully, conjuring images that may not yet exist in reality. A supportive environment enhances this creative process by allowing individuals to explore their inner landscapes without inhibition. Techniques such as guided imagery can be employed effectively in these spaces, helping individuals visualize their desired outcomes with clarity and intention.

Tips for Setting Up a Relaxing Environment

Creating a physical and mental safe space is essential for fostering relaxation, focus, and overall well-being. Here are some practical tips to help you design your sanctuary.

Choosing the Right Location

Quiet and Comfortable Setting

Select a location that feels peaceful and inviting. This could be a corner of your home, a cozy nook, or even a spot in a local park. The key is to choose a space where you can minimize interruptions and feel at ease. Ensure that the area is free from noise and distractions, allowing you to unwind and focus on yourself.

Designing Your Space

Calming Colors and Scents

Incorporate soothing colors like soft blues, greens, or neutrals into your decor. These hues can evoke feelings of tranquility. Additionally, consider using calming scents such as lavender or chamomile through candles or essential oils. Aromatherapy can significantly enhance your mood and create a serene atmosphere.

Soft Lighting

Lighting plays a crucial role in setting the tone of your space. Opt for soft, warm lighting instead of harsh fluorescents. Use lamps with dimmers or fairy lights to create a gentle glow that promotes relaxation. This can help signal to your brain that it's time to unwind.

Comforting Elements

Add cushions, blankets, and soft rugs to make your space inviting. These elements not only provide physical comfort but also contribute to a cozy ambiance. Incorporating plants can also enhance the environment; they improve air quality and add a touch of nature, which can be grounding.

Minimizing Distractions

Limit External Interruptions

To maintain focus in your safe space, turn off notifications on your devices and set boundaries with others about your time in this area. Consider using apps that block distracting websites or setting specific times when you check emails or social media.

Create a Routine
Establishing a routine for entering your safe space can signal to your mind that it's time to relax or focus. This could involve simple rituals like brewing a cup of tea, playing soft music, or practicing deep breathing exercises before you settle in.

Engaging Your Mind

Mindfulness Practices
Incorporate mindfulness techniques such as meditation or journaling into your routine within this space. These practices can help clear your mind of clutter and enhance your ability to focus on the present moment.

By thoughtfully designing your physical environment and creating intentional habits around it, you can cultivate a safe space that nurtures both your mental well-being and productivity.

How to use Visualization to Create a Sense of Safety and Security

When we visualize serene natural settings, such as a quiet beach with gentle waves lapping at the shore or a lush forest filled with the sounds of chirping birds, we engage our senses in a way that can evoke feelings of calm and tranquility. The vibrant colors of nature, the soothing sounds, and even the imagined scents of fresh pine or salty sea air can transport us to a place where we feel safe and at ease. This mental imagery activates the parasympathetic nervous system, which is responsible for relaxation, thereby counteracting stress responses in the body. For instance, picturing oneself sitting on a warm sandy beach, feeling the sun on their skin while listening to the rhythmic sound of waves, can significantly lower stress levels and promote peace of mind.

Similarly, visualizing a cozy room filled with comforting elements can enhance feelings of safety. Imagine a space adorned with soft pillows, warm lighting, and familiar scents—perhaps the aroma of vanilla or lavender from candles. This kind of imagery can evoke memories of home or cherished moments spent with loved ones. The colors chosen for this imagined space— soft blues, greens, or warm neutrals—can further enhance feelings of comfort and security. Research suggests that colors play a vital role in influencing mood; for example, blues and greens are often associated with tranquility and calmness. By regularly engaging in such visualization practices, individuals can create a mental refuge that they can return to whenever they need to alleviate stress.

Another effective technique involves recalling places that hold positive memories. This could be a childhood home filled with laughter or a favorite vacation spot where one felt completely relaxed. By vividly imagining these places—recalling specific details like the layout of the rooms, the sounds of laughter echoing through them, or the sights of beautiful landscapes—individuals can tap into feelings of nostalgia and warmth. This connection to positive memories not only provides immediate comfort but also reinforces a sense of belonging and safety within oneself.

Regular practice of these visualization techniques can strengthen this sense of safety over time. Just like any skill, visualization becomes more effective with repetition. By consistently returning to these peaceful mental images—whether it's through meditation, guided imagery exercises, or simply taking moments throughout the day to pause and visualize—individuals can train their minds to access feelings of calm more readily. This practice can create neural pathways that enhance emotional resilience against stressors.

Incorporating elements from nature into one's living space can further bolster this sense of security. For instance, adding indoor plants not only beautifies an environment but also connects individuals to nature—a concept known as biophilia—which has been shown to reduce stress levels significantly. The presence of greenery in one's surroundings fosters a calming atmosphere that complements the visualization practice.

Positive Affirmations

Positive affirmations serve as powerful tools for reshaping our mental landscape, offering a pathway to greater self-belief and emotional healing. At their core, affirmations are positive statements that challenge and counteract the negative self-talk many of us experience daily. This internal dialogue often stems from early life experiences and societal conditioning, embedding limiting beliefs deep within our psyche. By consciously repeating affirmations, we can begin to rewire our brains, shifting our focus from self-doubt to self-empowerment.

The psychological benefits of positive affirmations are profound. Research indicates that when we engage in affirmations, we activate the brain's reward system, which not only enhances our mood but also reduces feelings of emotional pain. This activation can alleviate stress and foster a sense of well-being, making it easier to navigate life's challenges. Affirmations essentially act as mental exercises; just as we train our bodies for physical strength, we can train our minds to cultivate resilience and positivity. Over time, this practice can lead to significant changes in how we perceive ourselves and our capabilities.

Moreover, affirmations play a crucial role in combating negative self-talk. Many individuals experience an overwhelming barrage of critical thoughts that can undermine their confidence and motivation. Affirmations serve as a counterbalance to this negativity, providing a mental switch that redirects focus toward more constructive beliefs. For instance, replacing thoughts like "I am not good enough" with "I am capable and deserving of success" can gradually shift one's self-image. This process is not merely about wishful thinking; it's about actively choosing to reinforce a healthier narrative about oneself.

The journey of using affirmations is also intertwined with the concept of self-compassion. When we practice affirmations that emphasize kindness towards ourselves, we create an environment conducive to healing and growth. Statements such as "I am worthy of love and respect" or "I embrace my journey with grace" encourage us to treat ourselves with the same compassion we would offer a friend in need. This nurturing approach helps dismantle the harsh judgments often imposed by our inner critic, fostering a more supportive internal dialogue.

Additionally, the repetitive nature of affirmations can help build resilience against life's adversities. By consistently affirming our strengths and capabilities, we cultivate a mindset that is better equipped to handle setbacks and challenges. This resilience is not just about bouncing back; it's about thriving despite difficulties. Each affirmation acts as a reminder of our inherent worth and potential, reinforcing the belief that we can overcome obstacles rather than being defined by them.

Positive affirmations are more than just phrases; they are transformative tools that empower us to reshape our thoughts and beliefs. They guide us in counteracting the negative narratives that often dominate our minds, promoting a healthier self-image and fostering resilience in the face of adversity. As we continue to practice these affirmations with intention and commitment, we embark on a journey toward greater self-acceptance and emotional well-being.

EFFECTIVE POSITIVE AFFIRMATIONS FOR TRAUMA RECOVERY

Embarking on the journey of trauma recovery can feel daunting, but positive affirmations can serve as a beacon of hope and strength. Here's a list of affirmations specifically crafted to empower you on your healing path:

I am safe and secure.

I am worthy of love and respect.

I choose to heal and grow stronger.

My past does not define my future.

I release the pain of my past and embrace
my present.

Every day, I am becoming more resilient.

I am deserving of joy and happiness.

I trust my journey and the process of healing.

I have the strength to face my fears.

My feelings are valid, and I honor them.

I am surrounded by love and support.

I forgive myself for any perceived shortcomings.

I am in control of my thoughts and emotions.

Each step I take is a step toward healing.

I am enough just as I am.

Personalizing Your Affirmations

While the above affirmations are powerful, personalizing them can amplify their impact on your healing journey. Here's how to tailor affirmations to fit your unique needs and experiences.

Reflect on Your Journey

Take a moment to think about your specific experiences with trauma. What feelings or beliefs have emerged as a result? Identifying these can help you create affirmations that resonate deeply.

Use "I" Statements

Start your affirmations with "I" to foster a sense of ownership and empowerment over your thoughts and feelings. For example, instead of saying, "You are strong," say, "I am strong."

Focus on Present Tense

Frame your affirmations in the present tense as if they are already true for you: "I am worthy" rather than "I will be worthy." This helps reinforce the belief in your current reality.

Be Specific

If there are particular aspects of your trauma or recovery that you want to address, make your affirmations specific to those areas. For instance, if trust is a challenge, you might say, "I trust myself to make safe choices."

Keep It Positive

Ensure that your affirmations focus on what you want to cultivate rather than what you want to avoid or eliminate. Instead of saying, "I am not afraid," try "I embrace courage in every situation."

Make It Personal

Incorporate elements that are meaningful to you—this could be values, goals, or even quotes that inspire you. For example, if family is important, you might say, "I nurture loving relationships with my family."

Practice Regularly

Repetition is key! Integrate these personalized affirmations into your daily routine—say them aloud in front of a mirror, write them in a journal, or meditate on them during quiet moments.

By personalizing your affirmations, you create a powerful tool that speaks directly to your heart and mind, guiding you through the complexities of trauma recovery with compassion and strength.

Feel free to adapt these suggestions further or ask for more examples tailored to specific experiences!

Incorporating Positive Affirmations into your Daily Routine

Integrating positive affirmations into your daily life can be a transformative experience, and it's all about creating a rhythm that feels natural and uplifting. One of the most effective ways to start is by setting aside specific times for your affirmations. Imagine beginning your day with a moment dedicated solely to yourself, where you can recite affirmations that resonate deeply with your goals and aspirations. Perhaps you choose to do this right after you wake up, allowing those positive thoughts to set the tone for the day ahead. Alternatively, you might find that a mid-morning break or an afternoon pause works better for you. The key is to find a time that feels right and stick with it, making it a cherished part of your routine.

Visual reminders can also play a crucial role in reinforcing your affirmations. Consider placing sticky notes with your favorite affirmations on your bathroom mirror, refrigerator, or workspace. These little nuggets of positivity will catch your eye throughout the day, gently nudging you back into that positive mindset whenever you need it. You might even create a vision board filled with images and words that inspire you, serving as a daily reminder of the affirmations you want to embody. The more you see these reminders, the more they become ingrained in your subconscious, helping to shift your mindset over time.

Incorporating affirmations into daily activities can seamlessly blend positivity into your life without requiring extra time or effort. For instance, during your morning routine, while brushing your teeth or washing your face, take a moment to repeat affirmations aloud or in your mind. You could say something like, "I am confident and capable," as you prepare for the day ahead. Meal times can also be an excellent opportunity for reflection; as you eat, consider expressing gratitude for your body and its abilities while affirming that you nourish it with love and care. Even before bed, as you wind down from the day's hustle and bustle, take a few moments to reflect on what went well and reaffirm your self-worth and intentions for tomorrow.

Consistency is paramount when it comes to making affirmations effective. The more regularly you practice them, the more they become part of your thought patterns. This doesn't mean you have to stick rigidly to a schedule; rather, find a flow that works for you and allows for flexibility. Life can be unpredictable, but even on days when everything feels chaotic, taking just a few minutes to recite your affirmations can anchor you back to a place of positivity.

Belief in the affirmations themselves is equally important. It's natural to feel skeptical at first—after all, changing long-held beliefs takes time and patience. Start with affirmations that feel achievable and gradually work up to bolder statements as your confidence grows. The process is about nurturing a sense of self-compassion; allow yourself grace as you navigate this journey. Remember that every time you repeat an affirmation, you're planting seeds of positivity in your mind, which will flourish with consistent care and attention.

Guided Imagery

Guided imagery is another powerful therapeutic technique that harnesses the mind's ability to create vivid mental images, promoting relaxation and aiding in emotional and physical healing. At its core, guided imagery involves visualizing serene and peaceful environments, which can significantly reduce stress and anxiety. This technique allows individuals to mentally transport themselves to tranquil settings—like a sunlit beach or a quiet forest—engaging all their senses in the process. The act of immersing oneself in these calming visuals can trigger a relaxation response in the body, lowering heart rates and blood pressure, thus counteracting the physiological effects of stress.

The benefits of guided imagery extend beyond mere relaxation. Research has shown that it can alleviate symptoms related to anxiety and depression. By focusing on positive mental images, individuals can shift their mindset away from negative thoughts that often exacerbate feelings of distress. This shift not only fosters a sense of calm but also encourages emotional resilience, allowing individuals to cope better with life's challenges. For instance, studies have indicated that patients who practice guided imagery report significant reductions in stress, fatigue, and pain levels, highlighting its effectiveness as a complementary approach to traditional therapies.

In the realm of trauma recovery, guided imagery serves as a valuable tool for healing emotional wounds. It provides a safe space for individuals to explore their feelings and experiences without being overwhelmed by them. By creating a mental sanctuary, those recovering from trauma can gradually confront difficult memories in a controlled manner. This process can facilitate emotional processing and help individuals reclaim their sense of safety and control. The technique allows for gradual exposure to distressing thoughts while simultaneously reinforcing feelings of comfort and security through visualization.

Moreover, guided imagery can be particularly beneficial for managing stress in high-pressure situations. Whether it's preparing for surgery or navigating daily life stresses, this technique equips individuals with the tools to calm their minds and bodies. Practicing guided imagery regularly helps establish a mental habit that can be accessed during moments of acute stress. Just as one might train their body for physical challenges, engaging in this mental practice prepares the mind to respond more effectively when faced with real-life stressors.

The beauty of guided imagery lies in its accessibility; it requires no special equipment or extensive training. Individuals can practice it anywhere—whether at home, in a quiet office corner, or even during a break at work. Guided imagery sessions can be self-directed or facilitated through audio recordings or apps designed to guide users through the process. This flexibility makes it an appealing option for those seeking effective stress management techniques.

Furthermore, the mind-body connection inherent in guided imagery underscores its potential for healing physical ailments as well. Studies have demonstrated that visualizing healing processes can lead to tangible improvements in conditions such as chronic pain or recovery from surgery. By mentally picturing their bodies healing or envisioning pain dissipating, individuals may experience reduced discomfort and enhanced recovery outcomes.

Guided imagery is more than just a relaxation technique; it is a multifaceted approach that promotes emotional well-being and physical health. By engaging the imagination and focusing on positive mental images, individuals can navigate stressors more effectively while fostering resilience against anxiety and trauma. As people continue to explore this therapeutic modality, its role in holistic health care becomes increasingly recognized and valued.

Examples of Guided Imagery Scripts for Trauma Recovery.

Here are examples of guided imagery scripts designed to guide listeners through peaceful environments, specifically focusing on a beach at sunset, a forest glade, and a mountain summit. Each script incorporates sensory details and positive affirmations to enhance the experience.

Beach at Sunset

Setting the Scene:
Begin by inviting the listener to find a comfortable position, either sitting or lying down. Encourage them to close their eyes and take a few deep breaths, inhaling calmness and exhaling tension.

Script:
"Imagine yourself standing on a soft, sandy beach. The sun is setting on the horizon, painting the sky with hues of orange, pink, and purple. Feel the warm sand beneath your feet as you take a step forward. As you walk, listen to the gentle waves lapping against the shore, creating a soothing rhythm.

Take a moment to breathe in the salty sea air. What do you smell? The faint scent of coconut oil from someone nearby? Or perhaps the fresh ocean breeze? Let these scents wash over you, bringing you peace.

As you gaze at the sunset, remind yourself: *I am safe. I am at peace. I deserve this moment of tranquility.* Allow these affirmations to resonate within you as the sun dips below the horizon."

Forest Glade

Setting the Scene:
Encourage listeners to visualize themselves in a lush forest glade, surrounded by tall trees and vibrant greenery.

Script:
"Picture yourself stepping into a serene forest glade. The sunlight filters through the leaves, casting playful shadows on the ground. As you walk deeper into this space, feel the cool earth beneath your feet and hear the soft rustle of leaves in the gentle breeze.

Pause for a moment and listen closely. Do you hear birds chirping or perhaps a distant stream flowing? Take a deep breath in—what does it feel like to inhale the fresh scent of pine and damp earth? With each breath, imagine inhaling calmness and exhaling any lingering stress.

Repeat quietly to yourself: *I am grounded. I am connected to nature. I embrace my healing journey.* Let these words fill your heart as you soak in this peaceful environment."

Mountain Summit

Setting the Scene:
Guide listeners to envision themselves at the summit of a majestic mountain, where they can see far and wide.

Script:
"Visualize yourself standing at the top of a magnificent mountain. The air is crisp and clear; every breath feels refreshing. As you look out over the valley below, notice how vast and beautiful the landscape is—rolling hills, sparkling rivers, and patches of forest.

Feel the strength in your legs from climbing this mountain. You have achieved something significant by reaching this height. Take a moment to appreciate your journey here.

As you stand tall against the wind, affirm to yourself: *I am strong. I have overcome challenges. I can rise above my fears.* Let these affirmations empower you as you take in this breathtaking view."

Sensory Details and Positive Affirmations

In each script:

- **Sensory Details:** Encourage listeners to engage all their senses—sight (colors), sound (waves or rustling leaves), smell (saltwater or pine), touch (sand or cool air)—to create an immersive experience.

- **Positive Affirmations:** Integrate affirmations that resonate with themes of safety, strength, and healing throughout each visualization. These should be simple yet powerful statements that listeners can repeat silently or aloud.

By leading listeners through these vivid imagery experiences with supportive language and affirmations, they can cultivate a sense of safety and empowerment crucial for trauma recovery.

Tips for Creating Your Own Guided Imagery Scripts

Crafting personalized guided imagery scripts is a deeply rewarding process that allows you to create unique experiences tailored to individual needs and preferences. The essence of guided imagery lies in its ability to engage the imagination, utilizing vivid and sensory details that transport the listener to serene and healing environments. By incorporating positive affirmations and ensuring that the script resonates with the listener's personal experiences, you can enhance the effectiveness of the imagery, making it a powerful tool for relaxation and transformation.

When beginning to write a guided imagery script, it's crucial to focus on **vivid and sensory details**. This means not only describing what the listener might see but also what they might hear, smell, feel, and even taste. For instance, if your imagery involves a tranquil beach, you could evoke the sound of gentle waves lapping against the shore, the warm sun on their skin, and the salty breeze in their hair. Such sensory engagement helps create a more immersive experience, allowing the listener's mind to fully embrace the journey you are guiding them through. The brain often struggles to distinguish between real and imagined experiences; therefore, the more detailed your descriptions, the more impactful the meditation will be.

Incorporating **positive affirmations** throughout your script serves as a gentle reminder of self-worth and potential. These affirmations can be woven into the narrative seamlessly; for example, as a listener imagines themselves walking along a peaceful forest path, you might suggest they affirm to themselves, "I am at peace with my surroundings" or "I embrace my journey with confidence." These statements not only promote relaxation but also encourage a positive mindset that can lead to lasting change.

To tailor your script effectively, start by considering the **individual needs and experiences** of your audience. Reflect on what they may be seeking from their meditation—whether it's stress relief, healing from trauma, or simply a moment of peace. This understanding will guide your choice of setting and imagery. For example, someone seeking comfort might resonate more with a cozy cabin in the woods rather than an expansive mountain vista. By aligning your script with their personal experiences and desires, you create a more meaningful connection that enhances their meditation experience.

Creating a guided imagery script can be approached through a step-by-step process. First, choose a **setting** that feels inviting and healing. This could be anything from a serene beach to a lush garden or even an imaginative realm unique to the listener's preferences. Once you've selected your setting, describe it in detail. Paint a picture with words that encompasses every sensory aspect—what colors dominate the landscape? What sounds fill the air? What scents linger? This rich description will help listeners visualize themselves within this comforting space.

Next, integrate **healing elements** into your script. This could involve visualizing light enveloping them for protection or imagining roots growing from their feet into the earth for grounding. Encourage listeners to breathe deeply and absorb these healing energies as they navigate through your guided imagery. By reinforcing feelings of safety and comfort throughout your script, you help foster an environment conducive to relaxation and healing.

As you write your script, remember that it should flow naturally. Use gentle transitions between sections to maintain a calming rhythm that guides listeners deeper into relaxation. It's beneficial to include pauses where participants can explore their inner experiences without feeling rushed. This allows them to connect more profoundly with their imagination and emotions during the meditation.

In summary, crafting personalized guided imagery scripts involves an artful blend of vivid sensory details, positive affirmations, and tailored content that resonates with individual experiences. By thoughtfully considering each element—from setting selection to integrating healing aspects—you create an enriching experience that supports relaxation and personal growth.

Visualization of Healing

Visualizing the body's healing from trauma involves a profound journey into the depths of our imagination, where the mind and body unite in a powerful dance of restoration. When we imagine our bodies repairing themselves, we engage in a process that transcends mere thought; it becomes an act of intention and belief. Picture yourself in a serene space, perhaps a quiet room or a lush garden, where you can focus solely on your healing. As you breathe deeply, allow your mind to conjure images of your body in its ideal state—strong, vibrant, and free from pain. This vivid imagery acts as a catalyst, awakening the body's innate ability to heal.

The process begins by acknowledging the sensations associated with trauma or pain. Rather than resisting these feelings, you can visualize them transforming into something more manageable. Imagine the pain as a dark cloud hovering over you, and with each exhale, picture that cloud dissipating into the air, leaving behind clarity and lightness. This technique not only reduces the immediate sensation of discomfort but also fosters a sense of control over your healing journey. By focusing on what you wish to feel—comfort, strength, and vitality—you actively redirect your body's energy towards recovery.

Visualization plays a crucial role in emotional healing as well. When we envision ourselves overcoming challenges, whether physical or emotional, we cultivate hope and resilience. This hopeful mindset is essential; studies have shown that positive visualization can increase serotonin levels in the brain, promoting feelings of well-being and relaxation. As you visualize your body regaining strength, imagine each muscle fiber knitting together seamlessly, each cell rejuvenating itself with energy and purpose. This mental exercise not only enhances your mood but also supports physiological processes that are vital for recovery.

Moreover, visualization can enhance immune function. Picture your immune system as an army of tiny warriors actively combating illness or injury. By visualizing this dynamic scene, you stimulate the production of immune-boosting substances like interleukins and lymphocytes. This mental imagery reinforces your body's defenses and accelerates the healing process. The more specific and vivid your visualization, the more effective it can be; envisioning details such as color or texture adds layers of depth that engage different senses and enhance the experience.

To effectively harness this power of visualization, it's beneficial to establish a routine. Set aside time each day for this practice—perhaps in the morning to set a positive tone for the day or at night to promote relaxation before sleep. Start by finding a comfortable position where you can close your eyes and breathe deeply. Allow yourself to drift into a state of calmness and then guide your thoughts towards healing imagery. Imagine inhaling pure light that fills your body with warmth and vitality while exhaling any negativity or tension.

As you immerse yourself in this visualization practice, remember that it is not merely about escaping reality but embracing it with intention. Each session is an opportunity to reconnect with your body's wisdom and resilience. Trust in this process; over time, you may find that not only does your physical condition improve but so does your emotional landscape. The journey of healing through visualization is one of empowerment—a reminder that within us lies an extraordinary capacity for renewal and growth.

Visualization Techniques for Healing Trauma

Visualization techniques can be powerful tools for healing trauma, providing a safe space for individuals to process emotions and experiences. Here are three effective techniques: the **Safe Place Visualization**, the **Healing Light Visualization**, and the **Balloon Release Visualization**. Each method offers unique benefits and can be practiced regularly to enhance emotional well-being.

SAFE PLACE VISUALIZATION

How It Works:

The Safe Place Visualization involves creating a mental image of a location where you feel completely secure and at ease. This place can be real or imaginary—a serene beach, a cozy room, or a tranquil forest. To practice, close your eyes and take several deep breaths, allowing yourself to relax. As you visualize your safe place, engage all five senses:

- **Sight:** What do you see? Colors, shapes, and details?
- **Sound:** Are there any sounds? The rustle of leaves, waves crashing, or soft music?
- **Touch:** What textures can you feel? The warmth of the sun or the coolness of grass?
- **Smell:** What scents are present? Fresh flowers or salty ocean air?
- **Taste:** Can you taste anything? Perhaps a refreshing drink or sweet fruit?

Benefits of Regular Practice:

Regularly practicing this visualization helps create a mental refuge that you can return to whenever stress or anxiety arises. It promotes relaxation, reduces anxiety levels, and enhances emotional resilience by reinforcing a sense of safety in your mind

HEALING LIGHT VISUALIZATION

How It Works:
In the Healing Light Visualization, you imagine a warm, healing light enveloping your body. Begin by finding a quiet space and closing your eyes. Visualize this light as a soft glow that starts at the top of your head and gradually moves down through your body. As it travels, it brings warmth and comfort to each area it touches, helping to release tension and negative emotions.

You might say to yourself affirmations such as "I am safe," "I am loved," or "I am healing" as the light flows through you. Allow yourself to feel any sensations that arise—perhaps warmth, tingling, or relaxation.

Benefits of Regular Practice:
This visualization not only fosters relaxation but also promotes self-compassion and healing. By regularly immersing yourself in this experience, you can cultivate a deeper connection with your body and emotions, allowing for greater healing over time

BALLOON RELEASE VISUALIZATION

How It Works:
The Balloon Release Visualization is a creative way to let go of negative emotions or worries. Start by imagining that you are holding a balloon in your hands. As you breathe deeply, visualize each worry or negative feeling being transferred into the balloon. You can choose the size and color of the balloon to represent different emotions.

Once you've filled the balloon with your worries, take a moment to tie it securely. Then, visualize releasing the balloon into the sky. Watch as it floats higher and higher until it becomes smaller and eventually disappears from view.

Benefits of Regular Practice:
This technique externalizes worries, making them feel more manageable. By visualizing them floating away, you give yourself permission to let go of anxiety associated with those feelings. Regular practice can lead to reduced stress levels and an enhanced sense of control over one's emotions.

These visualization techniques provide supportive methods for healing trauma by fostering emotional release and creating safe mental spaces for reflection and recovery.

Importance of Consistency in Visualization Practice

Regular and consistent practice in visualization is not merely a suggestion; it is a cornerstone of effective mental training that can profoundly impact both performance and well-being. Visualization, often described as a mental rehearsal, allows individuals to create vivid images and scenarios in their minds, engaging all five senses to bring their goals to life. However, the true power of this technique lies in its regular application. When practiced consistently, visualization becomes a skill that enhances its effectiveness over time. Just as athletes train their bodies through repetitive physical exercises, the mind also requires frequent workouts to strengthen its ability to visualize successfully.

The benefits of regular visualization extend beyond mere performance enhancement. Engaging in this practice consistently fosters a stronger mind-body connection, which is crucial for achieving holistic well-being. As individuals visualize their goals or desired outcomes repeatedly, they train their subconscious minds to recognize these visions as attainable realities. This process not only boosts confidence but also helps in reducing anxiety and stress, making it easier to navigate challenging situations. The more one practices visualization, the more natural it becomes to tap into this mental resource during high-pressure moments, ultimately promoting long-term healing and resilience.

To maintain a consistent visualization practice, setting a schedule is paramount. Just as one would block out time for physical training or other important activities, dedicating specific times for visualization helps establish it as a non-negotiable part of your routine. Whether it's first thing in the morning or right before bed, find a time that feels right for you and stick to it. Additionally, tracking your progress can be incredibly motivating. Consider keeping a journal where you note down your experiences after each session—what you visualized, how you felt, and any insights gained. This reflection not only reinforces your commitment but also allows you to see how far you've come over time.

Staying motivated can sometimes be the biggest challenge in maintaining consistency. One effective strategy is to create a vision board or use visual aids that resonate with your goals. These tangible reminders can serve as daily inspiration and keep your objectives at the forefront of your mind. Additionally, incorporating variety into your visualization practice can help keep it fresh and engaging. Experiment with different techniques—such as guided imagery or focusing on different senses—and allow yourself to adapt based on what feels most effective at any given time.

In this journey of visualization, remember that every small step counts. Embrace the process with patience and kindness toward yourself; the more you practice, the more adept you will become at harnessing the transformative power of visualization.

Cultivating Gratitude

Gratitude is a powerful emotion that can significantly enhance psychological and emotional well-being. When we consciously practice gratitude, we shift our focus from what we lack to appreciating what we have, which can lead to profound changes in our mental health. Research has  shown that engaging in gratitude practices can reduce stress and anxiety levels, leading to an immediate boost in happiness. For instance, a single act of expressing gratitude can yield a remarkable 10% increase in happiness and a 35% reduction in depressive symptoms, although these effects may diminish over time without continued practice. This highlights the importance of making gratitude a regular part of our lives, allowing us to cultivate a more positive emotional landscape.

The benefits of gratitude extend beyond mere mood enhancement; they also play a crucial role in overall well-being. Regularly acknowledging the good in our lives can lead to lower levels of stress hormones, creating a more balanced emotional state. This reduction in stress not only improves mood but also enhances various aspects of life, including sleep quality and interpersonal relationships.

Grateful individuals often report feeling more optimistic and engaged with their surroundings, which can foster resilience against life's challenges. By focusing on positive experiences, we train our brains to recognize opportunities rather than obstacles, promoting emotional resilience and better coping mechanisms when faced with adversity.

In the context of trauma recovery, gratitude serves as a vital tool for healing. It helps individuals reframe their experiences and find meaning even in difficult situations. By cultivating a mindset of gratitude, trauma survivors can begin to rebuild their sense of self-worth and connection to others. Studies indicate that people who practice gratitude are less likely to experience symptoms of major depression or anxiety disorders. This is particularly important for those recovering from trauma, as it allows them to focus on the positive aspects of their journey rather than being consumed by negative memories.

Moreover, gratitude fosters resilience by encouraging individuals to celebrate small victories and moments of joy amidst hardship. This practice not only boosts morale but also reinforces the belief that good things can happen even in challenging times. Writing about positive experiences or expressing thanks to others can create a ripple effect, enhancing social bonds and fostering a supportive community around individuals who are navigating their recovery journeys.

As we explore the emotional benefits of gratitude further, it becomes evident that this simple yet profound practice can transform lives. It encourages us to slow down and savor life's little moments, helping us stay grounded in the present rather than getting lost in worries about the future or regrets about the past. By actively engaging in gratitude, we not only improve our own well-being but also contribute positively to the lives of those around us, creating an environment where resilience and healing can flourish.

Ways to Practice Gratitude, Such as Keeping a Gratitude Journal or Expressing Gratitude to Others.

Practicing gratitude can transform your perspective and enhance your overall well-being, and there are several practical methods to incorporate this powerful practice into your daily life. One of the most effective ways to cultivate gratitude is through keeping a gratitude journal. This doesn't have to be a daunting task; in fact, it can be a delightful ritual. Set aside a few moments each day—perhaps in the morning with your coffee or at night as you wind down—to jot down three to five things you're grateful for. These can be as simple as the warmth of the sun on your skin or the kindness of a stranger. The key is to focus on specific moments rather than generalities; instead of writing "I'm grateful for my family," try "I'm grateful for the laughter we shared during dinner last night." This specificity not only deepens your appreciation but also helps you recall those moments vividly.

Expressing gratitude to others can be equally rewarding and is a wonderful way to strengthen relationships. A heartfelt thank-you note can go a long way in making someone feel valued and appreciated. Whether it's a friend who lent you an ear during a tough time or a colleague who helped you on a project, taking the time to articulate your appreciation can create ripples of positivity. You might find it helpful to set a goal of expressing gratitude to at least one person each week. This could be through a handwritten note, a thoughtful text, or even a face-to-face conversation where you share how their actions impacted you. The sincerity in your expression is vital; when people feel your genuine appreciation, it fosters deeper connections and encourages them to continue their acts of kindness.

Integrating gratitude into daily activities is another enriching approach. You can weave gratitude into routine tasks by simply pausing and reflecting on what you appreciate about that moment. For instance, while washing dishes, think about the food that nourished you, or when commuting, consider the safe travels that brought you to your destination. You might also create visual reminders around your home or workspace—sticky notes with affirmations or images that evoke feelings of gratitude can serve as prompts throughout your day. Even during challenging times, finding something small to appreciate can shift your mindset and help you navigate difficulties with more resilience.

Consistency is crucial in any gratitude practice. It's not just about having a few good days; it's about making gratitude a part of your lifestyle. By committing to these practices regularly, you'll start to notice shifts in how you perceive the world around you. The more consistently you acknowledge what you're thankful for, the more natural it becomes to see the positive amidst life's challenges. Sincerity plays an equally important role; when your expressions of gratitude come from an authentic place, they resonate deeply—not only with those around you but also within yourself. This authenticity fosters an inner sense of peace and fulfillment that enriches every aspect of life.

The Benefits of Gratitude for Reducing Stress and Anxiety

At its core, gratitude shifts our focus from what is lacking or negative in our lives to what is abundant and positive. This simple yet profound shift can rewire our brains, allowing us to cultivate a more optimistic outlook. When we consciously practice gratitude, we engage in a mental exercise that trains our brains to notice the good amidst the chaos. This is particularly crucial because anxiety often stems from a fixation on potential threats or negative outcomes. By redirecting our attention to positive experiences and emotions, we can effectively counteract the rumination that fuels anxiety.

The mechanisms behind gratitude's calming effects are rooted in both neurobiological and psychological processes. Research indicates that gratitude can reduce the production of stress hormones while enhancing overall well-being. When we express gratitude, whether through journaling or sharing our appreciation with others, we activate regions of the brain associated with reward and positive emotions. This activation not only fosters feelings of happiness but also helps regulate the autonomic nervous system, which plays a key role in managing our stress responses. In essence, gratitude acts as a natural antidote to the heightened arousal associated with anxiety, enabling us to experience a more balanced emotional state.

Moreover, gratitude cultivates a sense of abundance rather than scarcity. In times of uncertainty or distress, it's easy to feel overwhelmed by what we lack—be it security, health, or connection. Practicing gratitude encourages us to recognize and appreciate the resources we do have, whether they are supportive relationships, personal strengths, or simply the beauty of nature around us. This shift not only enhances our mood but also fosters resilience against stressors. By reinforcing our sense of connection to others and reminding us of our support systems, gratitude can buffer against feelings of isolation and helplessness that often accompany anxiety.

To harness the power of gratitude effectively in managing stress and anxiety, consider integrating it into your daily routine. Start by keeping a gratitude journal where you jot down three things you are thankful for each day. This practice doesn't have to be elaborate; even small acknowledgments can make a significant difference. Reflecting on these entries regularly can help reinforce positive thinking patterns over time. Additionally, take moments throughout your day to pause and appreciate simple joys—a warm cup of coffee, a kind word from a friend, or the beauty of a sunset. These mindful moments can ground you in the present and alleviate feelings of anxiety.

Another effective approach is to express your gratitude directly to others. Whether it's writing thank-you notes or verbally acknowledging someone's impact on your life, these acts not only strengthen your relationships but also enhance your own well-being. Sharing your appreciation creates a positive feedback loop; as you uplift others, you simultaneously elevate your own mood and sense of connection.

Incorporating gratitude into your life is not about ignoring pain or discomfort; rather, it is about embracing a holistic view that allows for both appreciation and acknowledgment of challenges. It's perfectly valid to feel anxious while also recognizing aspects of life that bring joy or comfort. This duality enriches our emotional experience and empowers us to navigate life's ups and downs with greater resilience.

By making gratitude a consistent part of your life, you can cultivate an inner landscape that is more conducive to peace and well-being. As you practice this transformative mindset, you may find that stressors become less daunting and that feelings of anxiety diminish in their intensity. Embracing gratitude is indeed a journey—a journey toward greater mental clarity, emotional stability, and an enriched life experience.

Chapter 3

Self-Regulation: Calming Your Nervous System

"The only way to heal is to feel." - Joanna Macy

Joanna Macy's profound wisdom resonates deeply in the realm of healing, particularly when it comes to understanding trauma and stress. She invites us to embrace our emotions fully, rather than suppressing or avoiding them. This perspective is crucial because healing is not merely about escaping discomfort; it is about engaging with our feelings, allowing ourselves to experience the full spectrum of human emotion. Macy eloquently states that our responses to the world's suffering—be it anger, grief, or despair—are rooted in our deep interconnectedness with all beings. These emotions are not signs of weakness but rather indicators of our compassion and humanity. By acknowledging and processing these feelings, we can begin to mend not only ourselves but also our relationship with the world around us.

Self-regulation plays a pivotal role in this healing journey. It involves recognizing and managing our emotional and physical responses to stress, allowing us to navigate through life's challenges with greater resilience. This process requires us to cultivate awareness of our internal states and learn how to respond rather than react impulsively. Self-regulation is not about denying or minimizing our feelings; instead, it empowers us to face them head-on, fostering a sense of agency in our healing process. By practicing self-regulation, we can create a safe space for ourselves where we can explore our emotions without judgment or fear.

As we delve into the techniques for achieving self-regulation, it becomes clear that these practices serve as powerful tools for healing. Techniques such as mindfulness meditation, breathwork, and grounding exercises help us reconnect with our bodies and emotions. They encourage us to slow down and tune into the present moment, allowing us to process what we feel rather than becoming overwhelmed by it. This chapter will guide readers through various methods designed to enhance self-regulation skills, emphasizing that these practices are not just beneficial but essential for anyone seeking to heal from trauma and stress.

Macy reminds us that the act of being present—of showing up for ourselves and others—is a radical form of love that can transform both individual lives and the collective experience. In this light, self-regulation emerges as a practice of compassion towards oneself, enabling us to hold space for our pain while simultaneously fostering hope for healing. As we embark on this exploration together, let us embrace the journey of feeling deeply as a pathway toward liberation and connection, recognizing that in facing our emotional truths, we open doors not only for personal growth but also for collective healing.

Identifying Triggers

The physical manifestations of stress and anxiety can be profound and often overwhelming, serving as a reminder of the body's intricate response to perceived threats. When faced with stressors, whether they are immediate dangers or chronic worries, our bodies engage in a series of physiological changes known as the fight-or-flight response. This automatic reaction is rooted in our evolutionary past, designed to prepare us for survival by either confronting or fleeing from danger.

One of the most noticeable symptoms of this response is an **increased heart rate**, or tachycardia. As the body prepares to either fight or flee, adrenaline surges into the bloodstream, causing the heart to pump faster and more forcefully. This heightened state ensures that vital organs receive more blood and oxygen, priming the body for action. Alongside this, **rapid breathing** occurs as the lungs work harder to take in oxygen, further fueling the muscles and brain for quick responses. Individuals may find themselves breathing shallowly or hyperventilating, which can exacerbate feelings of anxiety.

Another common physical manifestation is **muscle tension**. The body instinctively tightens muscles in preparation for potential physical exertion. This tension can lead to discomfort and pain if it persists over time, contributing to a cycle of stress and physical discomfort. Additionally, **sweating** often increases as the body attempts to cool itself down in anticipation of exertion. This can be particularly distressing in social situations, where excessive sweating may be perceived as a sign of nervousness or fear.

Digestive issues frequently accompany stress and anxiety as well. The body prioritizes functions essential for immediate survival, often diverting blood away from the digestive system. This can lead to symptoms such as nausea, stomach cramps, or even diarrhea. These reactions highlight how interconnected our emotional states are with our physical well-being; when we feel threatened or anxious, our bodies react accordingly.

Understanding these responses is crucial because they are part of a complex system aimed at keeping us safe. The fight-or-flight mechanism is an evolutionary adaptation that has allowed humans and other animals to survive potentially life-threatening situations. However, when this response is triggered too frequently—such as during non-threatening situations like public speaking or meeting deadlines—it can lead to chronic stress and anxiety disorders. In such cases, the body remains in a heightened state of alertness that can be detrimental to both mental and physical health.

To navigate these challenges more effectively, it's essential to become attuned to our bodies' signals. One helpful practice is maintaining a **journal** that tracks physical sensations alongside emotional states. By documenting experiences when symptoms arise—like increased heart rate or muscle tension—individuals can begin to identify patterns and triggers related to their stress responses. This awareness can empower people to implement coping strategies tailored to their needs.

Additionally, incorporating mindfulness techniques such as deep breathing exercises or progressive muscle relaxation can help mitigate the physical effects of anxiety. These practices encourage individuals to reconnect with their bodies in a calming way, fostering a sense of control over their physiological responses. By tuning into these signals and responding with self-care techniques, individuals can better manage their stress and anxiety levels while promoting overall well-being.

Common Triggers for Trauma Flashbacks and Panic Attacks

Understanding the triggers that can lead to trauma flashbacks and panic attacks is essential for anyone navigating the complexities of post-traumatic stress disorder (PTSD) or complex PTSD (C-PTSD). These triggers can be broadly categorized into internal and external stimuli, each capable of activating the nervous system and eliciting intense emotional and physical responses.

Internal triggers often manifest as thoughts, memories, or emotions that are reminiscent of the traumatic event. For instance, a person may experience a sudden wave of anxiety when recalling a distressing memory, such as an accident or an assault. This recollection can evoke feelings of fear, helplessness, or shame that were present during the original trauma. Such emotional responses can lead to physiological reactions like increased heart rate, sweating, or even dissociation, where one feels detached from their body or surroundings. Emotional flashbacks, characterized by overwhelming feelings such as sadness or abandonment without clear visual or auditory cues, can also be triggered by everyday situations that unconsciously remind someone of past trauma. For example, receiving criticism might evoke feelings of inadequacy rooted in childhood experiences of neglect or abuse.

On the other hand, external triggers are often more tangible and can include sounds, smells, places, or even specific people that are associated with the traumatic experience. A loud noise might remind a combat veteran of gunfire, triggering a flashback that feels as though they are reliving the event. Similarly, a particular scent—perhaps cologne worn by an abuser—can provoke visceral reactions and memories tied to the trauma. Locations can also serve as powerful reminders; for someone who experienced a traumatic event in a specific setting, returning to that place can elicit panic attacks or intense emotional distress. The anniversary of a traumatic event often acts as an external trigger as well, bringing forth memories and feelings that can overwhelm an individual.

The activation of the nervous system in response to these triggers is rooted in the body's survival mechanisms. When confronted with reminders of past trauma, the brain perceives these stimuli as threats, activating the fight-or-flight response. This response floods the body with stress hormones like cortisol and adrenaline, preparing it for immediate action. However, for individuals with PTSD or C-PTSD, this system can become hyperactive; they may experience heightened states of alertness or panic even in safe environments. The resulting panic attacks can be debilitating and accompanied by symptoms such as chest pain, shortness of breath, dizziness, and a profound sense of impending doom.

Recognizing personal triggers is a vital step toward healing. Keeping a journal to document experiences surrounding flashbacks or panic attacks can help individuals identify patterns and contexts in which these reactions occur. Understanding these triggers not only aids in managing reactions but also fosters self-compassion and insight into one's emotional landscape. It is essential to approach this exploration with patience and kindness toward oneself; uncovering these triggers is not merely an exercise in self-awareness but a journey towards reclaiming one's narrative and sense of safety in the world.

Relaxation Techniques:

Progressive Muscle Relaxation (PMR) is a powerful technique designed to promote both physical and mental relaxation. Developed by Dr. Edmund Jacobson in the 1920s, PMR is based on the premise that physical relaxation can lead to mental calmness. This method involves systematically tensing and then relaxing different muscle groups throughout the body, helping individuals become more aware of their physical sensations and reducing stress.

To begin practicing PMR, find a quiet and comfortable space where you can either sit or lie down without distractions. It's beneficial to wear loose clothing and take a moment to settle into your chosen position. Start by taking several deep breaths, inhaling through your nose and exhaling through your mouth. This initial focus on your breath sets the stage for relaxation and helps clear your mind.

The process of PMR starts at your feet. Begin by curling your toes tightly for about five seconds while inhaling deeply. Feel the tension build in your toes and feet, then release the tension suddenly as you exhale, allowing your feet to relax completely. Spend a few moments noticing the difference between the tension and the relaxation. This awareness is crucial as it helps you recognize how tension manifests in your body.

Next, move on to your calves. Tense these muscles by pointing your toes toward you while holding your breath for a few seconds. Then, release and feel the relaxation wash over you as you exhale. Continue this pattern as you work your way up through each muscle group: tighten your thighs, squeeze your buttocks, and contract your abdominal muscles, following the same rhythm of tensing and releasing.

As you progress to your upper body, tense your hands into fists, hold for a moment, and then let go. Move up to your arms, pulling them toward your shoulders as if making a muscle. Feel the tension build before releasing it completely. Next, focus on your shoulders; lift them toward your ears and hold before letting them drop down in a relaxing sigh.

Transitioning to the neck and face, gently tilt your head back while tensing the neck muscles, then relax. Squeeze your eyes shut tightly and purse your lips together before releasing all tension from these areas. Finally, finish with deep breathing while focusing on any residual tension in the forehead or jaw.

Throughout this process, deep breathing plays an essential role. Inhale deeply when tensing each muscle group and exhale fully when relaxing them. This synchronized breathing not only enhances the relaxation response but also helps anchor your awareness in the present moment.

The benefits of PMR are extensive. Regular practice can significantly reduce muscle tension, lower heart rate, and promote an overall sense of calmness. Research has shown that PMR can alleviate symptoms of anxiety and stress while improving sleep quality and even helping with chronic pain management. By incorporating PMR into your routine—ideally for 10 to 20 minutes each day—you can cultivate a greater awareness of bodily sensations and learn to identify when you're holding tension unnecessarily.

Encouragingly, PMR is accessible to everyone; it requires no special equipment or extensive training, making it an ideal tool for enhancing overall well-being. As you practice regularly, you'll likely find it easier to tap into this state of relaxation whenever needed, fostering resilience against life's stresses while nurturing both body and mind.

Yoga Nidra

A Guided Relaxation Technique That Promotes Deep Rest and Healing.

Yoga nidra, often referred to as "yogic sleep," is a transformative guided relaxation technique that invites practitioners into a profound state of rest and healing. The practice begins with finding a comfortable position, typically lying on your back in **Corpse Pose** (Shavasana). This position allows the body to fully surrender to the ground, promoting a sense of safety and relaxation. To prepare for your session, it's beneficial to choose a quiet space where you won't be disturbed. You might want to dim the lights and use a blanket for added comfort.

As you settle in, close your eyes and take a few deep breaths, letting go of any tension or distractions from your day.

Once you're comfortable, the guided meditation begins. The instructor will lead you through a process known as body scanning, where you focus your awareness on each part of your body sequentially. Starting from your right foot, you'll direct your attention there for a few moments, consciously relaxing it before moving up to your knee, thigh, and hip. This process continues through each part of your body—right leg, left leg, torso, arms, neck, face, and head—allowing you to cultivate a deep sense of relaxation and awareness. The beauty of yoga nidra lies in its ability to keep you in a state of conscious awareness while guiding you toward deep relaxation; it's not about falling asleep but rather about entering a restful state that rejuvenates both body and mind.

The benefits of yoga nidra are extensive. Many practitioners find that it significantly reduces stress levels by activating the parasympathetic nervous system, which promotes a state of calm and relaxation. This practice can help alleviate symptoms of anxiety and depression while improving overall emotional well-being. By regularly engaging in yoga nidra, individuals often report better sleep quality and an enhanced ability to manage daily stressors. The practice encourages self-awareness and introspection, allowing individuals to confront and process emotions without becoming overwhelmed.

Incorporating yoga nidra into your self-care routine can be as simple as setting aside 20-40 minutes a few times a week. There are numerous resources available for guided sessions that cater to various needs and preferences. You can find free guided meditations on platforms like YouTube or through dedicated meditation apps. For those new to the practice or seeking structured guidance, consider exploring programs like "Effortless Yoga Nidra," which offer comprehensive introductions to this restorative technique.

A Gentle Form of Exercise That Combines Movement, Breathing, and Meditation.

Tai chi, often referred to as "meditation in motion," is a gentle yet profoundly impactful form of exercise that harmonizes movement, breathing, and meditation. Rooted in ancient Chinese martial arts, tai chi emphasizes slow, flowing movements that cultivate both physical and mental well-being. This practice is not just about physical exertion; it invites practitioners to engage deeply with their breath, enhancing the connection between mind and body. As you move through its graceful postures, you will find that each motion is accompanied by deep, diaphragmatic breathing, which serves to ground you and promote a sense of tranquility.

At the heart of tai chi are its guiding principles: the focus on slow and deliberate movements encourages mindfulness and present-moment awareness. Each sequence flows seamlessly into the next, creating a meditative rhythm that calms the mind while invigorating the body. The breathing techniques integral to tai chi are designed to facilitate the exchange of energy; inhaling during expansive movements and exhaling during contractions fosters a natural flow of life energy throughout the body. This synchronization of breath and movement not only enhances relaxation but also promotes better oxygenation of the body, which can help reduce stress hormones like cortisol.

The physical benefits of tai chi are extensive. Regular practice can lead to improved balance and flexibility, making it an excellent choice for individuals of all ages and fitness levels. Research indicates that tai chi can enhance proprioception—the body's ability to sense its position in space—thereby reducing the risk of falls, particularly among older adults. Furthermore, it has been shown to alleviate pain and stiffness associated with various conditions such as arthritis and enhance overall well-being for those managing chronic illnesses like type 2 diabetes. Mentally, tai chi serves as a powerful tool for stress reduction; its meditative aspects help quiet the mind and foster emotional resilience.

For those new to tai chi, finding a supportive environment is key. Consider joining a local class or searching for online tutorials that resonate with you. Many community centers or gyms offer introductory sessions where you can learn from experienced instructors who can guide you through the foundational movements safely. If you prefer practicing at home, instructional videos can provide valuable insights into the flow of movements and breathing techniques. Remember, tai chi is highly adaptable; whether you are standing or seated, there are modifications available to accommodate various physical abilities.

As you embark on your tai chi journey, embrace the process with an open heart and mind. Allow yourself to explore this gentle yet powerful practice as a means of promoting self-regulation and enhancing your overall health. With patience and consistency, you may find that tai chi not only enriches your physical capabilities but also nurtures your mental clarity and emotional balance.

Emotional Regulation

The relationship between emotions and the body is a profound and intricate one, revealing how deeply intertwined our mental and physical states truly are. Emotions are not merely abstract feelings; they manifest as tangible physical sensations that can be felt throughout the body. When we experience joy, for instance, we might feel a rush of energy, a lightness in our step, or even a warmth spreading through our chest. Conversely, emotions like anxiety can tighten our muscles, create a lump in our throat, or induce a churning sensation in our stomachs. This connection is often referred to as the mind-body connection, illustrating how our emotional experiences trigger physiological responses that prepare us to face various environmental challenges.

Research has shown that different emotions correspond to specific patterns of bodily sensations. For example, studies have created maps that illustrate where people feel different emotions in their bodies. Participants reported sensations associated with basic emotions such as fear, anger, and happiness, highlighting consistent patterns across cultures. Fear typically leads to increased heart rate and muscle tension, while happiness may create a sense of lightness and relaxation throughout the body. This phenomenon suggests that emotions are represented not just in our minds but also within our somatic systems, as our bodies respond to emotional stimuli in ways that can be both profound and universal.

Consider anxiety: it often manifests physically through muscle tension and an elevated heart rate. When faced with a stressful situation—like an important presentation—many people experience tightness in their shoulders or a racing heart. These sensations are not mere side effects; they serve as signals from the body that something is amiss, prompting us to take action or seek relief. On the other hand, when we engage in relaxation techniques such as deep breathing or meditation, we may notice a significant shift in our emotional state. These practices can help release built-up tension and promote a sense of calmness and clarity.

The feedback loop between emotions and physical sensations is powerful. For instance, when someone feels sad or depressed, they might notice changes in their posture—slumped shoulders or a downcast gaze—which can further perpetuate feelings of sadness. Conversely, adopting an open posture or smiling—even when we don't feel particularly happy—can sometimes elevate our mood. This interplay illustrates how our physical state can influence our emotional experience just as much as our emotions can affect our physical sensations.

Mindfulness and body awareness practices offer valuable tools for exploring this connection further. By tuning into our bodies and becoming aware of how we physically experience emotions, we can cultivate greater emotional intelligence. Techniques such as body scans or mindful movement encourage us to listen to what our bodies are telling us. For instance, during moments of stress or anxiety, taking time to notice where we feel tension can help us identify the underlying emotions at play. This awareness can empower us to address those feelings more effectively.

Healthy Ways to Express and Process Emotions.

Healthy emotional expression and processing are essential for maintaining our mental well-being. The journey begins with acknowledging our feelings, whether they arise from joy or sorrow, anger or fear. One effective strategy is **journaling**, which provides a safe space to explore thoughts and emotions without judgment. Writing allows us to articulate feelings that might otherwise remain unexpressed, offering clarity and insight into our emotional landscape. As we put pen to paper, we can reflect on our experiences, identify patterns, and even uncover underlying issues that may need addressing.

Engaging in conversations with trusted friends or therapists can also be a powerful way to process emotions. Talking about what we feel helps to externalize those emotions, making them more manageable. A supportive friend can provide perspective, while a therapist can guide us through deeper emotional work. Both avenues encourage vulnerability and foster connections that remind us we are not alone in our struggles.

Creative activities, such as art or music, serve as another avenue for emotional expression. These forms of creativity allow us to channel feelings into something tangible, whether it's through painting, playing an instrument, or even dancing. Engaging in creative pursuits can be incredibly cathartic; they enable us to express complex emotions that words might fail to capture. This process not only provides relief but also promotes self-discovery and personal growth.

Setting boundaries is crucial in emotional health as well. It's important to communicate our needs effectively, ensuring that we protect our emotional space and prioritize self-care. Boundaries help us navigate relationships more healthily by allowing us to express what is acceptable and what isn't. This practice fosters mutual respect and understanding in our interactions with others.

When it comes to managing difficult emotions like anger, sadness, and fear, several strategies can be beneficial. First, **mindfulness** plays a significant role in emotional regulation. By becoming aware of our feelings without judgment, we can observe them rather than react impulsively. This practice encourages us to sit with our emotions, acknowledging their presence without the pressure to change them immediately. For instance, when feeling anger rise within us, rather than lashing out or suppressing it, we can take a moment to breathe deeply and reflect on what triggered that emotion.

Self-compassion is another vital aspect of processing difficult feelings. Instead of criticizing ourselves for experiencing negative emotions, we should treat ourselves with the same kindness we would offer a friend in a similar situation. This shift in perspective allows us to validate our experiences and reduces the tendency to spiral into guilt or shame.

Additionally, it's essential to identify the root cause of our emotions. When we feel sadness or fear, asking ourselves questions like "What am I truly afraid of?" or "What is the source of this sadness?" can help clarify our feelings and guide us toward constructive action. Naming these emotions diminishes their power over us; it transforms overwhelming feelings into manageable concepts that we can address.

Lastly, practicing positive self-talk is crucial when navigating challenging emotions. Instead of succumbing to negative narratives—like "I should have handled this better"—we can reframe our thoughts into more supportive statements such as "I am doing my best" or "It's okay to feel this way." This practice not only alleviates emotional distress but also fosters resilience in the face of adversity.

Mindfulness Techniques for Managing Difficult Emotions

Mindfulness is a powerful practice that encourages a non-judgmental awareness of the present moment, allowing us to engage with our thoughts and feelings without becoming overwhelmed by them. At its core, mindfulness invites us to observe our emotions as they arise, acknowledging their presence without labeling them as good or bad. This approach fosters a deeper understanding of our emotional landscape, enabling us to manage difficult emotions more effectively. When we practice mindfulness, we cultivate an environment where emotions can be felt and processed rather than suppressed or ignored.

One of the most accessible mindfulness techniques is focusing on the breath. This practice involves taking a moment to breathe deeply and intentionally, paying attention to each inhalation and exhalation. As thoughts and feelings arise, the goal is not to push them away but to acknowledge them and gently return focus to the breath. This simple act can serve as an anchor during turbulent emotional times, helping to ground us in the present moment. Similarly, body scan meditation is another effective technique where individuals mentally scan their bodies from head to toe, noticing areas of tension or discomfort. This practice not only promotes relaxation but also enhances body awareness, allowing us to connect physical sensations with emotional experiences.

Loving-kindness meditation is yet another valuable mindfulness practice that can be particularly beneficial for managing difficult emotions. This technique involves silently repeating phrases that express goodwill and compassion towards oneself and others. By cultivating feelings of love and kindness, we can soften the edges of negative emotions such as anger or resentment. This practice fosters a sense of connection with ourselves and others, reminding us that we are not alone in our struggles.

The benefits of incorporating mindfulness into our daily lives are profound. Research has shown that regular mindfulness practice can lead to increased emotional resilience, enabling individuals to bounce back more quickly from setbacks. It has also been linked to reduced stress levels, improved focus, and enhanced overall well-being. By learning to observe our emotions without judgment, we gain clarity and perspective that can transform how we respond to life's challenges. Mindfulness helps us recognize that emotions are temporary; they ebb and flow like waves in the ocean. This understanding empowers us to navigate difficult feelings with greater ease.

To truly reap the benefits of mindfulness, it's essential to practice regularly. Just as physical exercise strengthens the body, consistent mindfulness practice cultivates mental clarity and emotional stability. By dedicating time each day—whether through meditation, mindful breathing exercises, or simply being present during daily activities—we can develop a greater sense of inner peace and control over our emotional responses. Embracing mindfulness as a supportive tool in our lives allows us to face challenges with a calm heart and an open mind, fostering resilience in the face of adversity.

Grounding and Centering

Grounding techniques play a vital role in fostering present-moment awareness and emotional stability, especially in our fast-paced, often overwhelming lives. These methods serve as anchors, helping us to redirect our focus from distressing thoughts and feelings back to the here and now. By engaging our senses and bodily awareness, grounding techniques can effectively calm anxiety and promote a sense of control amidst chaos.

One of the most popular grounding techniques is the **5-4-3-2-1 method**. This exercise invites you to identify five things you can see, four things you can touch, three things you can hear, two things you can smell, and one thing you can taste. This sensory engagement not only distracts from anxious thoughts but also immerses you in your immediate environment, allowing you to appreciate the details that often go unnoticed. For instance, while observing your surroundings, you might notice the intricate patterns on a rug or the gentle sway of a tree outside your window. This simple act of observation helps to create a mental space where anxiety cannot thrive.

Deep breathing is another foundational grounding technique that is both accessible and effective. When feelings of overwhelm arise, focusing on your breath can be transformative. By taking slow, deep breaths—inhaling through the nose and exhaling through the mouth—you engage your body's relaxation response. This practice not only calms the nervous system but also brings your attention back to your body, reinforcing your connection to the present moment. As you breathe deeply, pay attention to how each breath feels as it fills your lungs and how it feels to release it. This mindful breathing creates a rhythm that can soothe racing thoughts and restore emotional balance.

Physical movement also serves as a powerful grounding technique. Engaging in activities like walking, stretching, or even dancing allows for a release of pent-up energy and tension. Movement encourages blood flow and can shift your focus from internal turmoil to the sensations in your body—how your feet feel against the ground or how your muscles stretch and contract. Even something as simple as standing up and shaking out your limbs can help reset your emotional state and reconnect you with the physical world around you.

Incorporating these grounding techniques into daily life not only aids in managing acute stress but also cultivates a habit of mindfulness that enhances overall emotional resilience. The beauty of these practices lies in their simplicity; they require no special equipment or extensive training, making them accessible for anyone seeking relief from anxiety or emotional distress. By practicing these techniques regularly—even when you're not feeling overwhelmed—you build a toolkit that prepares you for life's inevitable challenges. Through this supportive approach, grounding techniques empower individuals to reclaim their sense of agency and presence in an ever-changing world.

Centering Exercises to Connect with Your Body and Calm your Mind

Centering exercises serve as a powerful bridge to connect with our bodies and cultivate a calm, focused mind. These practices invite us to slow down, breathe deeply, and tune in to our physical sensations, creating a sanctuary of mindfulness amidst the chaos of daily life. Among the most effective centering exercises are the **3-Part Breath**, the **Roots Visualization**, and the **Body Scan**. Each of these techniques offers unique benefits that enhance our overall well-being while reducing stress and improving focus.

The **3-Part Breath**, also known as Dirga Pranayama, is a foundational breathing exercise that allows us to engage fully with our breath and body. To practice this technique;

- Find a comfortable position, either seated or lying down.
- Begin by closing your eyes and taking a moment to notice your natural breath without altering it.

This initial step helps quiet the mind and prepares you for deeper engagement. The first phase involves inhaling deeply through your nose, directing the breath into your belly. Feel it expand like a balloon; then exhale slowly, drawing your navel toward your spine to release all the air. After several cycles of this deep belly breathing, move to phase two: inhale into your belly again, then allow the breath to rise into your ribcage, feeling it widen. Exhale from the ribs first before releasing the breath from your belly. Finally, in phase three, fill your upper chest after the belly and ribcage are full. As you exhale, let the air escape from your chest, then ribs, and finally belly. This structured breathing not only calms the mind but also stimulates the parasympathetic nervous system, promoting relaxation and reducing anxiety.

Another effective exercise is the **Roots Visualization**, which helps ground you in the present moment. Imagine roots growing from the soles of your feet into the earth beneath you. As you visualize these roots extending deeper into the ground, feel a sense of stability and support arising from this connection. This imagery can evoke feelings of safety and calmness, making it easier to release tension and anxiety. By focusing on this grounding sensation, you create a mental anchor that helps you remain present and centered.

The **Body Scan** is another powerful centering practice that invites awareness to each part of your body while promoting relaxation. Begin by lying down comfortably or sitting in a relaxed position. Close your eyes and take a few deep breaths to settle in. Starting from your toes and moving upward through each part of your body, focus on any sensations you feel—tightness, warmth, or tingling—and consciously release any tension as you exhale. This practice not only enhances body awareness but also fosters a deeper connection between mind and body.

Engaging in centering exercises like these brings numerous benefits that extend beyond mere relaxation. They can significantly reduce stress levels by activating the body's relaxation response, which counteracts stress hormones and promotes feelings of calmness. Additionally, these practices improve focus by training the mind to concentrate on specific sensations or breathing patterns rather than getting lost in distractions or racing thoughts. Over time, regular practice can lead to enhanced overall well-being, including better emotional regulation and increased resilience against life's challenges.

Through these simple yet profound exercises, we learn to reconnect with our bodies and cultivate a sense of inner peace that can transform our daily experiences. By integrating centering practices into our routines, we not only enhance our mental clarity but also nurture our physical health—creating a holistic approach to well-being that empowers us to navigate life with grace and ease.

Combining Grounding and Centering for Optimal Self-Regulation

Combining grounding and centering techniques can significantly enhance self-regulation, allowing individuals to better manage their emotions, thoughts, and behaviors. Grounding techniques help anchor you in the present moment, providing a sense of stability and safety. Centering techniques, on the other hand, focus on cultivating inner calm and clarity, enabling you to respond thoughtfully rather than react impulsively. By integrating these practices into your daily routine, you can create a powerful framework for optimal self-regulation.

To start your day effectively, consider beginning with a grounding exercise. This could be as simple as taking a few moments to focus on your breath. Find a comfortable position, close your eyes, and take deep breaths—inhale slowly through your nose, hold for a moment, and exhale gently through your mouth. As you breathe, pay attention to the sensations in your body and the sounds around you. This practice not only helps center your thoughts but also brings awareness to your physical presence in the here and now. You might also try grounding yourself by feeling the texture of an object in your hand or visualizing roots extending from your feet into the earth, connecting you to a stable foundation.

As your day progresses, remember that self-regulation is an ongoing process. Throughout the day, you may encounter stressors that challenge your emotional balance. When these moments arise, take a brief pause to engage in a grounding technique again. This could involve stepping outside for fresh air or practicing mindful walking—focusing on each step and how it feels against the ground beneath you.At the end of the day, implement a centering exercise to reflect on your experiences and emotions. Find a quiet space where you can sit comfortably without distractions. Close your eyes and visualize a serene place that brings you peace—this could be a beach, forest, or any space that feels safe and calming. Allow yourself to immerse in this visualization while focusing on your breath. With each inhale, imagine drawing in calmness; with each exhale, let go of any tension or stress accumulated throughout the day.

Consistency is key when integrating these practices into your life. Just like any skill, developing effective self-regulation takes time and patience. It's essential to show up for yourself daily, even when it feels challenging or when immediate results are not visible. Much like nurturing a plant—where growth is not always immediately apparent—you must trust that with consistent effort and care, positive changes will manifest over time.

Encourage yourself to experiment with various grounding and centering techniques to discover what resonates most with you personally. Some may find solace in meditation or journaling, while others might prefer physical activities like yoga or tai chi. The goal is to make self-regulation an integral part of your self-care routine—something that nourishes both your mind and body.

As you embark on this journey of self-regulation through grounding and centering practices, remember that setbacks are part of the process. Embrace them as opportunities for growth rather than reasons to abandon your efforts. Each day presents a new chance to refine these skills and deepen your understanding of yourself. With patience and dedication, you'll find that these techniques not only enhance your ability to manage stress but also enrich your overall well-being.

Seeking Support

The journey of trauma recovery is often laden with challenges, but one of the most critical components that can significantly ease this path is a strong support system. Having supportive relationships can lead to increased resilience, reduced feelings of isolation, and an overall improvement in emotional well-being. When individuals experience trauma, they may feel as though they are navigating their pain alone, which can exacerbate feelings of despair and hopelessness. However, the presence of understanding friends, family members, or community groups can provide a vital buffer against these negative emotions. Supportive relationships foster a sense of belonging and connection, allowing individuals to share their experiences and feelings without fear of judgment. This shared experience not only validates their struggles but also reinforces the idea that they are not alone in their journey.

Building a support system is essential for anyone recovering from trauma. One effective way to start is by reaching out to friends and family. These connections can serve as a safe haven where individuals feel seen and heard. Engaging in open conversations about feelings and experiences can help dismantle the walls of isolation that trauma often erects. Additionally, joining support groups can be incredibly beneficial. These groups provide a space for individuals to connect with others who have faced similar challenges, creating an environment rich in empathy and understanding. Sharing stories in these settings can be cathartic and empowering, as participants realize that their feelings are not only valid but also shared by others.

In today's digital age, connecting with online communities can also play a significant role in recovery. Many platforms offer forums where individuals can discuss their experiences anonymously, providing a level of comfort that may be difficult to achieve in face-to-face settings. These online spaces often cultivate supportive networks that extend beyond geographical boundaries, allowing individuals to find solace and encouragement from people worldwide.

Mutual support is a cornerstone of healing from trauma. The act of sharing experiences creates bonds that can lead to deeper understanding and compassion among individuals. When someone shares their story of pain, it opens the door for others to do the same, fostering an atmosphere where healing becomes a collective endeavor rather than a solitary struggle. This interconnectedness not only helps reduce the stigma surrounding trauma but also encourages individuals to lean on one another during difficult times.

Moreover, the power of shared experiences cannot be overstated. When people come together to discuss their traumas, they often discover common threads in their stories that highlight resilience and strength. This recognition can be profoundly uplifting, instilling hope and motivation for recovery. It reinforces the idea that while trauma may shape our lives, it does not define them; rather, it is how we respond and connect with others that truly matters.

Finding Supportive Relationships and Communities

Finding supportive relationships and communities is essential for emotional well-being and personal growth. One of the most effective ways to start this journey is by seeking out local support groups or online forums that resonate with your interests and challenges. These spaces provide a sense of belonging and understanding, where you can share experiences and learn from others facing similar situations. Whether it's a group focused on mental health, parenting, or hobbies, being part of a community can significantly enhance your support network.

Participating in therapy or counseling sessions is another powerful avenue for building connections. A therapist can not only help you navigate personal challenges but also guide you in developing healthier relationships. They can assist in identifying patterns that may be hindering your ability to connect with others and provide strategies to foster more meaningful interactions. Engaging in these sessions often leads to greater self-awareness, which is crucial when it comes to forming supportive relationships.

Setting boundaries is an integral part of establishing healthy connections. Boundaries help define what is acceptable in your interactions with others and protect your emotional space. They are not walls that isolate you but rather fences that allow you to engage fully without compromising your well-being. Communicating your needs effectively is key to this process. Using "I" statements can help express your feelings without placing blame on others, making it easier for them to understand your perspective. For instance, saying "I feel overwhelmed when…" can open up a dialogue about how to adjust the relationship dynamics in a way that feels comfortable for you.

In addition to local resources, there are numerous online platforms designed to connect individuals seeking support. Websites such as Meetup or Eventbrite often list local gatherings, workshops, and support groups tailored to various interests and needs. Apps like BetterHelp or Talkspace provide access to licensed therapists from the comfort of your home, making it easier than ever to prioritize your mental health. Community centers frequently host events and programs aimed at fostering connections among residents, so be sure to explore those options as well.

Taking the first step toward building a support network can feel daunting, especially if you're unsure where to start. However, it's crucial to remember that every small effort counts. Whether it's reaching out to a friend for coffee or joining an online discussion group, each action brings you closer to creating the supportive environment you deserve. Embrace the discomfort that may arise from stepping out of your comfort zone; it's often a sign of growth and an opportunity for new connections.

Professional Help for Complex Trauma: Therapists, Support Groups, and Other Resources

Seeking professional help for complex trauma is an essential step towards healing and recovery. Complex trauma, often resulting from prolonged exposure to distressing events such as childhood abuse or domestic violence, can deeply affect an individual's emotional and psychological well-being. The journey through trauma can feel overwhelming, and navigating this path alone may lead to feelings of isolation and despair. This is where therapists, counselors, and other mental health professionals play a crucial role in providing specialized support.

Therapists and counselors create a safe and supportive environment where individuals can explore their feelings, thoughts, and reactions related to their traumatic experiences. They offer empathetic listening and non-judgmental guidance, helping clients make sense of their emotions and experiences. This therapeutic relationship is vital; it fosters trust and encourages individuals to confront their trauma in a secure space. Mental health professionals utilize various therapeutic approaches tailored to the unique needs of each individual, recognizing that there is no one-size-fits-all solution for trauma recovery.

Among the effective therapies available for treating complex trauma are cognitive-behavioral therapy (CBT), eye movement desensitization and reprocessing (EMDR), and somatic experiencing. CBT focuses on identifying and changing negative thought patterns that contribute to emotional distress. It empowers individuals to develop coping strategies that allow them to manage their symptoms effectively. EMDR, on the other hand, helps individuals process traumatic memories by using guided eye movements while recalling distressing events. This technique aims to reduce the emotional charge associated with these memories over time, facilitating healing. Somatic experiencing takes a different approach by focusing on the body's sensations and responses to trauma. It emphasizes the importance of bodily awareness in processing traumatic experiences, helping individuals reconnect with their physical selves.

Support groups also play a significant role in the recovery process for those dealing with complex trauma. These groups provide a platform for individuals to share their experiences and connect with others who have faced similar challenges. This shared understanding fosters a sense of community and reduces feelings of isolation, enabling participants to learn from one another's coping strategies. Support groups can be particularly beneficial because they create an environment where vulnerability is met with empathy and encouragement.

In addition to therapy and support groups, various resources are available for those in crisis or seeking immediate assistance. Hotlines and crisis services offer confidential support from trained professionals who can provide guidance during moments of acute distress. These resources are crucial for individuals who may feel overwhelmed or unsure about taking the first step towards seeking help.

Encouragingly, reaching out for professional help is not a sign of weakness but rather a courageous step towards reclaiming one's life after trauma. It signifies a commitment to healing and self-discovery, allowing individuals to process their experiences in a constructive manner. Professional support equips individuals with the tools necessary to manage their symptoms, rebuild their lives, and foster resilience against future challenges. If you or someone you know is struggling with trauma, consider seeking help from qualified mental health professionals; it could be the pivotal moment on the path toward recovery and empowerment.

HOPE ANDRUS

Chapter 4

Body Scan Techniques: Tuning In to Your Body

"The body is a wise and faithful guide." - Alice Walker

A full-body scan is a powerful foundational practice in mindfulness and relaxation, serving as a bridge between the mind and body. This technique encourages individuals to cultivate awareness of their physical sensations, helping to identify areas of tension that may often go unnoticed in our fast-paced lives. By engaging in this practice, we can develop a deeper connection with our bodies, allowing us to recognize and address discomfort or stress before it escalates.

As we embark on this journey of self-discovery, it's essential to approach the body scan with an open heart and a willingness to explore. The process begins by finding a comfortable position, either lying down or seated, ensuring that your body is supported and at ease. Close your eyes gently and take a moment to focus on your breath. Inhale deeply through your nose, allowing your abdomen to rise, and then exhale slowly through your mouth, visualizing any tension melting away with each breath. This rhythmic breathing will serve as your anchor throughout the scan.Start at your toes, directing your attention to this often-overlooked area. Notice any sensations present—perhaps a tingling feeling or tightness in the muscles. Allow yourself to breathe into this area, imagining each inhale bringing warmth and relaxation while each exhale releases any tension. After spending a moment here, gently shift your focus to the soles of your feet, then to your heels and ankles. Continue this gradual ascent up your legs, paying close attention to the calves, knees, and thighs. With each body part you scan, take time to acknowledge any discomfort or tightness without judgment.

As you move up to your hips and pelvis, observe how these areas feel in relation to the rest of your body. Are they relaxed or tense? Breathe deeply into these regions, visualizing tension dissipating with every exhale. Transitioning to the abdomen, notice the rise and fall of your belly as you breathe. Is there tightness or ease? Allow yourself to simply be present with these sensations.

Next, bring awareness to your chest. Feel the expansion as you inhale and the gentle contraction as you exhale. Acknowledge how this area feels emotionally—are there feelings of anxiety or calm? Continue this process with your shoulders, arms, and hands. Pay attention to each finger individually if you wish; notice any sensations like warmth or coolness.

As you reach your neck and throat, check for any tightness that may have accumulated from stress or tension throughout the day. Breathe deeply into this area, imagining it softening with each breath out. Finally, direct your focus to your head—the crown down through the forehead, eyes, cheeks, jaw, and back of the head. Allow yourself to feel fully present in this moment.

Throughout this entire process, remember that breath plays a crucial role in releasing tension. Each deep inhale brings in fresh energy while each slow exhale helps release what no longer serves you. If thoughts begin to drift away from the scan, gently guide them back without frustration; this practice is about cultivating awareness rather than achieving perfection.

As you complete the scan from toes to crown, take a few moments to sit with this awareness of your entire body—feel how it is connected and how sensations flow throughout. This practice not only fosters relaxation but also enhances self-awareness and promotes emotional well-being by creating space for acceptance and understanding of our physical selves.

Different Body Parts and Noticing any Areas of Discomfort or Tightness

Recognizing and paying attention to subtle sensations in our bodies can be a transformative practice, especially when it comes to understanding areas of discomfort or tightness. Our bodies often hold tension in specific areas as a response to stress, past trauma, or the repetitive motions of daily activities. This tension can manifest in various ways, and by becoming attuned to these sensations, we can begin to unravel the underlying causes and facilitate healing.

Many individuals experience tension in common areas such as the shoulders, neck, and lower back. The shoulders are particularly notorious for holding stress;

they often bear the weight of our responsibilities and emotional burdens. When we feel overwhelmed or anxious, it's not uncommon for us to unconsciously tighten our shoulders, leading to discomfort and pain. This phenomenon is aptly captured in the saying about "carrying the weight of the world on your shoulders." By acknowledging this tension, we can start to explore what emotions or pressures we might be internalizing.

The neck is another area where tension frequently accumulates. It is closely linked to our ability to express ourselves and communicate effectively. When we feel fear or anxiety, particularly regarding self-expression or vulnerability, our neck muscles may contract as a protective mechanism. This can lead not only to physical discomfort but also to a sense of being stifled or unable to articulate our thoughts and feelings. Engaging with this area through gentle exploration can reveal insights into our emotional state and help us release pent-up feelings.

Lower back tension is often associated with feelings of guilt, shame, or unworthiness. This area can become a repository for unresolved emotions and past traumas, making it essential to approach it with curiosity rather than judgment. When we take the time to notice sensations in our lower back—whether they manifest as tightness, warmth, or coolness—we open ourselves up to understanding the deeper emotional narratives at play.

As you gently explore these areas of tension, approach them with a sense of curiosity. Allow yourself to notice any sensations without labeling them as good or bad. You might feel warmth radiating from your muscles or perhaps a tingling sensation that signals an area needing attention. It's important to create a space where you can observe these feelings without self-criticism; this non-judgmental awareness is crucial for fostering healing and relaxation.

Incorporating practices such as deep breathing or mindful stretching can further enhance your connection with your body. These techniques not only promote relaxation but also encourage blood flow and flexibility in tense areas. As you breathe deeply, visualize the breath flowing into areas of tightness, allowing them to soften and release. This conscious engagement with your body can create a profound shift in how you experience discomfort and tension.

Using Breath and Visualization to Promote Relaxation and Healing.

Engaging in breathwork and visualization can profoundly enhance your body scan experience, promoting relaxation and healing. One of the most effective techniques to incorporate is **diaphragmatic breathing**, also known as deep or belly breathing. This method focuses on using the diaphragm, a dome-shaped muscle located at the base of the lungs, to facilitate deeper and more efficient breathing. When you breathe deeply, your abdomen expands as you inhale, allowing for a fuller exchange of oxygen and carbon dioxide. This not only helps to lower your heart rate and blood pressure but also activates the body's relaxation response, counteracting stress and anxiety. As you practice this technique, you may notice a gentle warmth spreading through your body, a sign that your muscles are relaxing and your mind is calming.

To practice diaphragmatic breathing effectively, find a comfortable position—either sitting or lying down.

Place one hand on your chest and the other on your abdomen. Inhale slowly through your nose for about four seconds, feeling your belly rise while keeping your chest relatively still. Hold this breath for a moment before exhaling slowly through pursed lips for about six seconds. This rhythmic pattern not only encourages relaxation but also serves as a distraction from racing thoughts, allowing you to focus solely on the sensations of breathing. With regular practice, diaphragmatic breathing can become an effortless tool in your self-care toolkit.

In conjunction with breathwork, visualization exercises can further enhance your relaxation experience. Imagine a warm, healing light enveloping your body as you breathe in deeply. Visualize this light flowing through you with each inhalation, illuminating any areas of tension or discomfort. As you exhale, picture this warm light dissolving the tension away, leaving behind a sense of peace and tranquility. This imagery can create a powerful connection between your mind and body, reinforcing the calming effects of your breath.

Another effective visualization technique involves picturing each breath as a gentle wave of relaxation washing over you. With every inhalation, imagine this wave beginning at the soles of your feet, gradually rising up through your legs and torso, enveloping your arms and shoulders before finally reaching the crown of your head. As this wave flows through you, it carries away any stress or discomfort, leaving you feeling lighter and more at ease. By combining these breathing techniques with visualization exercises, you cultivate an environment conducive to deep relaxation and healing.

Targeted Scans

The concept of targeted scans, particularly in the context of mindfulness and body awareness, serves as a powerful tool for addressing specific areas of the body that may be holding tension or unresolved emotions. This practice involves a focused attention technique where individuals mentally scan their bodies, often from head to toe, to identify areas of discomfort, pain, or emotional heaviness. By bringing awareness to these regions, such as the chest, stomach, or jaw, one can begin to understand how trauma and stress manifest physically. This connection between emotional experiences and bodily sensations is crucial; it highlights how unresolved emotions can become stored in the body, leading to chronic tension and discomfort.

Trauma can be stored in various ways within the body. When individuals experience distressing events, their bodies often react by tightening muscles or creating physical barriers as a protective mechanism. Over time, these responses can lead to persistent tension in specific areas. For instance, the chest may feel tight due to anxiety or grief, while the stomach might hold feelings of fear or insecurity. The jaw can also be a common area of tension, often associated with stress or frustration. Recognizing these patterns is essential for healing; targeted scans allow individuals to gently explore these sensations without judgment.

Engaging in targeted scans encourages a compassionate approach to self-exploration. As you begin this practice, it's vital to approach each area with gentleness and curiosity rather than force or expectation.

Start by finding a comfortable position—whether sitting or lying down—and take a few deep breaths to center yourself. Gradually bring your attention to one area at a time. For example, if you focus on your chest, notice any sensations present: Is there tightness? A feeling of heaviness? Allow yourself to breathe into that space, visualizing the breath as a gentle wave that soothes and releases tension.

As you move through your body during the scan, pay particular attention to any emotions that arise. It's not uncommon for feelings such as sadness or anger to surface when focusing on areas that have held trauma. Acknowledge these emotions without trying to change them; simply observe their presence and allow them to coexist with your physical sensations. This process fosters a deeper understanding of your body's responses and helps create a safe space for healing.

Identifying these areas of tension is an ongoing journey. You may find that certain spots consistently draw your attention over time. Keeping a journal can be beneficial; jot down your observations after each scan session. This practice not only enhances self-awareness but also creates an opportunity for reflection on how your emotional state may influence physical sensations.

Ultimately, the goal of targeted scans is not just about alleviating physical discomfort but also about cultivating a compassionate relationship with your body. By approaching these practices with kindness and patience, you empower yourself to release stored energies and foster a deeper sense of well-being. Embrace this journey as one of self-discovery and healing, allowing each scan to guide you toward greater awareness and acceptance of both your physical and emotional selves.

Using Targeted Scans to Release Stored Emotions and Sensations

Understanding the intricate relationship between physical tension and emotional states reveals a profound truth: our emotions are not merely abstract feelings; they manifest as tangible sensations within our bodies. This connection often goes unnoticed, yet it plays a crucial role in our overall well-being. Emotions such as stress, anxiety, or sadness can create physical symptoms—tightness in the chest, knots in the stomach, or tension in the shoulders. These sensations are signals from our body, indicating that something needs attention. When we ignore these signals, we risk storing unresolved emotions, which can lead to chronic physical discomfort and emotional distress.

Releasing these stored emotions is essential for emotional healing. Techniques such as deep breathing, progressive muscle relaxation, and guided visualization serve as effective tools for this process. Deep breathing encourages a state of calm and helps to release pent-up energy. By inhaling deeply through the nose and exhaling slowly through the mouth, you can create a sense of relaxation that permeates your entire being. This simple act allows you to focus on the present moment while gently coaxing your body to release tension.

Progressive muscle relaxation takes this a step further by guiding you to systematically tense and then relax each muscle group in your body. This practice not only helps to identify areas of tension but also fosters a deeper awareness of how emotions are physically expressed. As you progress through each muscle group—from your toes to your head—you may discover where you hold emotional weight, allowing for a conscious release of that stored energy.

Guided visualization is another powerful technique that can facilitate emotional release. By imagining a safe space or a calming scenario, you create an environment conducive to exploring your feelings. During this practice, visualize any emotions that arise as colors or shapes; this can help externalize what might feel overwhelming when kept internal. As you visualize these emotions, consider what they might need from you—acknowledgment, expression, or even a farewell.

Mindfulness plays an integral role throughout this journey of emotional release. By cultivating self-awareness and acceptance of your feelings without judgment, you allow yourself to experience emotions fully rather than suppressing them. Practicing mindfulness encourages you to sit with discomfort and recognize the sensations in your body associated with various emotions. This process of recognition is vital; it opens the door to understanding what those sensations are trying to communicate.

As you engage in these techniques, it's important to approach any emotions that arise with self-compassion. Emotions can be intense and complex; allowing yourself to feel them without judgment creates a safe space for healing. When feelings surface during your practice, take a moment to acknowledge them. Ask yourself what these emotions are trying to tell you and how they relate to your physical sensations. This dialogue between mind and body fosters a deeper connection and understanding of your emotional landscape.

Exploring and expressing these emotions can be liberating. Whether through journaling about your experiences or engaging in creative outlets like art or movement, finding ways to articulate what you're feeling is crucial for processing stored emotions. Remember that this journey is not linear; it requires patience and kindness toward yourself as you navigate through layers of emotion and sensation.

Incorporating these techniques into your daily routine can lead to profound shifts in how you experience both your physical body and emotional state. The path to healing is uniquely personal; what resonates with one person may differ for another. Therefore, remain curious about what practices feel right for you and allow yourself the freedom to explore various methods of release. As you embark on this journey of self-discovery and healing, know that each step taken toward releasing stored emotions brings you closer to a more integrated and harmonious existence.

Combining Targeted Scans with other Relaxation Techniques

Integrating targeted scans with other relaxation techniques can create a harmonious and effective approach to enhancing overall well-being. Targeted scans, often used in mindfulness practices, involve focusing attention on specific areas of the body to release tension and promote relaxation. When combined with techniques such as yoga, meditation, or aromatherapy, the benefits can be amplified, leading to a more profound sense of calm and awareness.

Incorporating yoga into your routine alongside targeted scans can be particularly beneficial. Yoga combines physical postures, breath control, and meditation, which can deepen the body awareness achieved through targeted scans. For instance, during a restorative yoga session, you might begin with a targeted scan of your body while in a gentle pose. As you focus on areas of tension, you can consciously breathe into those spaces, allowing the breath to facilitate release. This practice not only enhances your physical flexibility but also fosters a deeper connection between your mind and body.

Meditation is another powerful ally when paired with targeted scans. By engaging in a body scan meditation, you systematically bring awareness to different parts of your body, noticing any sensations without judgment. To enhance this experience, consider using essential oils known for their calming properties. For example, diffusing lavender essential oil while performing a body scan can create an atmosphere conducive to relaxation. The soothing scent of lavender can help quiet the mind and deepen your meditative state, allowing you to fully immerse yourself in the practice.

Aromatherapy can further enrich both yoga and meditation practices. Imagine setting up your yoga space with a diffuser filled with eucalyptus oil before starting your routine. The invigorating scent not only freshens the air but also helps clear the mind and energize the body as you move through your poses. Similarly, after completing a targeted scan or meditation session, applying a few drops of chamomile oil to pulse points can enhance feelings of tranquility and promote restful sleep.

Encouraging experimentation is essential in finding the right combination of techniques that resonate with you personally. Perhaps you might discover that practicing a targeted scan followed by a few minutes of mindful breathing while inhaling essential oils creates a uniquely calming experience. Alternatively, integrating visualization techniques during your scans—imagining tension melting away like ice in the sun—can also add a layer of depth to your relaxation routine.

Ultimately, the journey toward relaxation is highly individualistic. By exploring various combinations of targeted scans with practices like yoga, meditation, and aromatherapy, you can uncover what works best for you. Allow yourself the freedom to experiment with different scents and techniques; whether it's using peppermint oil for an energizing yoga flow or indulging in sandalwood during evening meditations, each practice holds the potential to enhance your relaxation experience profoundly.

Movement and Sensation

Incorporating movement into body scan practices can significantly enhance the overall experience, offering a deeper connection between mind and body. The body scan itself is a mindfulness technique that encourages individuals to bring awareness to various parts of their body, noting sensations without judgment. However, when gentle movements are integrated into this practice, they can help release built-up tension and improve circulation, creating a more holistic approach to mindfulness.

Movement plays a crucial role in alleviating physical and emotional stress. As we engage in gentle stretches or yoga poses, we activate our muscles and joints, which can lead to the release of pent-up tension. This release not only fosters relaxation but also promotes better blood flow throughout the body. Improved circulation can enhance oxygen delivery to tissues and aid in the removal of metabolic waste, contributing to an overall sense of well-being. For instance, as you progress through a body scan, you might pause at each area of focus to incorporate a gentle stretch or movement. By doing so, you allow your body to express its needs and respond to sensations more fully.

Examples of gentle movements that can be seamlessly integrated into a body scan include simple stretches like reaching your arms overhead while focusing on your shoulders or gently twisting your torso while concentrating on your spine. These movements encourage a sense of fluidity and openness in the body. Yoga poses such as Child's Pose or Cat-Cow can also be effective; they not only stretch the muscles but also invite mindfulness into the movement itself. For those who prefer a more dynamic approach, walking meditation offers an excellent opportunity to connect with the ground beneath you while remaining aware of your body's sensations.

As you explore these various movements during your body scan practice, take note of how they affect your body and mind. You might find that certain movements feel particularly nurturing or healing, while others may bring up discomfort or resistance. This exploration is an essential part of the process; it encourages self-discovery and fosters a compassionate relationship with your body. By tuning into how different movements resonate with you, you cultivate an environment where healing can occur naturally.

Ultimately, the integration of movement into body scan practices invites a more profound engagement with oneself. It transforms the experience from mere observation to active participation in one's own healing journey. As you experiment with different movements, remember that there is no right or wrong way to do this—what matters most is finding what feels good for you and allowing yourself the grace to explore this nurturing path.

Paying Attention to The Sensations in Your Body as You Move

Movement is an intrinsic part of being human, yet in the hustle and bustle of daily life, we often find ourselves moving on autopilot. We rush from one place to another, our minds occupied with thoughts about the past or future, while our bodies perform actions mechanically. This disconnect can lead to a sense of fatigue, stress, and even physical discomfort. However, when we embrace mindfulness during movement, we can cultivate a profound awareness that enriches both our physical and mental well-being. By paying attention to the sensations in our bodies as we move, we deepen the connection between mind and body, allowing for a more harmonious experience of life.

Imagine taking a moment to pause and notice how your feet feel as they touch the ground. Each step can become a dance of awareness, where you feel the texture of the surface beneath you—the coolness of grass or the firmness of pavement. As you walk, allow your attention to drift to the subtle shifts in your weight, the way your muscles engage and release with each stride. This simple act of tuning into your feet can transform a mundane walk into a meditative practice. It invites you to experience movement not just as a means to an end but as an opportunity for connection and discovery.

As you continue to move, shift your focus to the sensations coursing through your body. Notice the stretch in your muscles as you reach for something overhead or bend down to tie your shoes. Feel how your body responds to these movements—perhaps there's a gentle pull in your hamstrings or a warm release in your shoulders. By acknowledging these sensations, you create a dialogue between your mind and body that fosters greater awareness and understanding. This connection can help alleviate tension and promote relaxation, encouraging you to move with greater ease and grace.

Breath is another vital aspect of mindful movement that deserves attention. As you engage in physical activity—whether it's yoga, dancing, or simply walking—pay close attention to how your breath flows in tandem with your movements. Inhale deeply as you lift your arms overhead, feeling the expansion in your chest and abdomen. Exhale fully as you fold forward, releasing any lingering tension. This rhythmic interplay between breath and movement not only enhances physical performance but also calms the mind, grounding you in the present moment.

To cultivate this mindfulness further, try setting an intention before you begin moving. It could be as simple as "I will be aware of my body" or "I will embrace each sensation." Allow this intention to guide you as you move through space. As you engage in activities throughout your day—whether it's stretching in the morning or taking a leisurely stroll—keep returning to this intention. Notice how each movement affects not only your body but also your emotional state. Do certain actions bring joy or relief? Are there movements that trigger discomfort or resistance? By observing these responses without judgment, you create an opportunity for growth and self-discovery.

Moving with intention means being present in every action you take. It invites curiosity into your experience; instead of merely going through the motions, ask yourself how each movement feels and what it brings up for you emotionally and physically. This practice can be especially beneficial during exercise routines or sports activities where it's easy to get caught up in performance metrics or outcomes. Instead of focusing solely on speed or strength, embrace the sensations—the rush of adrenaline, the burn in your muscles, or even the fatigue that follows an intense workout. Each feeling is a part of your journey toward greater self-awareness.

By integrating mindfulness into movement, we open ourselves up to a richer experience of life—one where we are fully engaged with our bodies and present in each moment. The beauty lies not just in achieving fitness goals but in savoring the process itself—the gentle sway of your hips as you dance or the satisfying stretch after a long day at work. Each movement becomes an invitation to connect more deeply with yourself, fostering a sense of peace and fulfillment that resonates beyond physical activity into every facet of life.

Using Movement to Release Tension and Promote Healing

Movement serves as a profound and accessible means of releasing tension and promoting healing in both body and mind. When we engage in movement, we activate our muscles, stimulate circulation, and encourage the release of endorphins—our body's natural stress relievers. This process not only alleviates physical discomfort but also fosters emotional well-being, creating a holistic approach to health.

Consider simple yet effective movements such as **shoulder rolls**, which can significantly relieve tension in the neck and shoulders. By gently rolling your shoulders forward and backward, you help to loosen tight muscles that often accumulate stress from daily activities, such as sitting at a desk or carrying heavy bags. This movement encourages blood flow to the area, promoting relaxation and reducing stiffness. Similarly, **hip circles** are fantastic for targeting the lower back, an area where many people experience chronic tension. By standing with feet hip-width apart and making circular motions with your hips, you not only stretch the muscles around the pelvis but also enhance mobility in the lower back, allowing for a greater range of motion and relief from discomfort.

Incorporating regular movement into your daily routine can create a more balanced body. It doesn't require lengthy sessions at the gym; even short bursts of activity can yield significant benefits. For instance, taking a few minutes for gentle stretching or a brisk walk during breaks can reset your body's tension levels. Activities like yoga or tai chi emphasize slow, deliberate movements that promote mindfulness while simultaneously releasing muscle tightness. These practices encourage you to connect with your body, enhancing awareness of where you hold tension and how to let it go.

Additionally, consider the power of **shaking therapy**, which involves shaking different parts of your body to release built-up stress and tension. This technique can be as simple as standing up and shaking out your arms and legs for a minute or two. It's an excellent way to bring attention back to your body while also engaging the nervous system in releasing pent-up energy. As you shake, focus on your breath—inhale deeply and exhale fully—allowing any residual tension to dissipate with each breath.

The beauty of movement lies in its adaptability; it can be tailored to fit any lifestyle or fitness level. Whether you're a seasoned athlete or just starting out, finding joy in movement is key. Perhaps you enjoy dancing in your living room or gardening on weekends; these activities not only keep you active but also nurture your spirit. Remember that even small actions count—taking the stairs instead of the elevator or doing a few stretches while watching television can make a difference.

As you begin to weave movement into your everyday life, pay attention to how it affects your overall sense of well-being. Notice how your body feels before and after engaging in these practices; this awareness can motivate you to continue exploring different forms of movement that resonate with you. The journey toward releasing tension through movement is personal and unique for everyone, but the rewards—a more relaxed body and a clearer mind—are universally beneficial.

Embracing Discomfort

Discomfort often emerges as a significant component in the body scan process, serving as a vital signal from our bodies that something requires our attention. When we engage in body scan meditation, we cultivate a heightened awareness of our physical sensations, allowing us to notice areas of tension or discomfort that we might otherwise overlook in our daily lives. This practice encourages us to confront these sensations rather than dismiss them, fostering a deeper understanding of our physical and emotional states. Discomfort can indicate areas where we may be holding stress or unresolved emotions, acting as an invitation to explore these feelings more fully.

Acknowledging and tolerating discomfort is crucial for personal growth and healing. Many people instinctively shy away from uncomfortable sensations, viewing them as negative experiences to be avoided. However, this avoidance can perpetuate a cycle of disconnection from our bodies and emotions. By learning to tolerate discomfort, we open ourselves up to valuable insights about our well-being. It becomes a tool for self-discovery; instead of seeing discomfort as an enemy, we can reframe it as a guide that leads us towards areas needing care and attention.

To navigate discomfort effectively, several strategies can be employed. Deep breathing is one such method; it helps ground us and brings calmness to the body. By focusing on slow, intentional breaths, we can create space within ourselves to observe discomfort without judgment. Mindfulness practices further enhance this experience by encouraging us to remain present with our sensations, observing them as they are without the need to change them. This non-judgmental awareness allows us to develop a more compassionate relationship with ourselves.

Self-compassion plays a pivotal role in how we handle discomfort. Instead of criticizing ourselves for feeling pain or unease, we can practice kindness towards ourselves during these moments. This shift in perspective fosters resilience and nurtures emotional well-being. When discomfort arises, approaching it with curiosity—

asking ourselves what it might be trying to communicate—can transform our experience from one of fear to one of exploration.

Engaging with discomfort through body scan meditation can be an enriching journey if approached with an open mind. Each session becomes an opportunity not just to identify pain but also to understand its origins and implications for our overall health. By embracing discomfort as part of the human experience, we empower ourselves to grow beyond it, learning valuable lessons about our bodies and minds along the way.

Gradual Exposure to Uncomfortable Sensations

Gradual exposure is a powerful technique that helps individuals build tolerance to uncomfortable sensations, fears, or anxieties. The essence of this approach lies in the principle that repeated, controlled exposure to discomfort can significantly reduce the fear and anxiety associated with it. When we confront what makes us uneasy in a structured manner, we allow our bodies and minds to adapt, ultimately leading to desensitization. This process not only diminishes the intensity of our fear responses but also fosters a sense of empowerment as we learn that we can manage discomfort effectively.

The journey of gradual exposure begins with recognizing your discomfort and understanding that it is a natural part of the process. Imagine dipping your toes into a chilly pool; the initial shock can be overwhelming, but with each moment spent in the water, your body acclimates. Similarly, by starting with mild discomfort and progressively increasing its intensity, you can train your mind and body to tolerate situations that once felt daunting. This method is akin to training a muscle; it requires consistency and patience but yields significant strength over time.

To embark on this journey, first identify a specific sensation or situation that you find uncomfortable. Begin by creating a hierarchy of fears related to this discomfort. For example, if you have a fear of public speaking, your list might start with imagining yourself speaking in front of a small group, then progressing to practicing in front of friends, and eventually addressing a larger audience. Each step should be manageable; the goal is to ensure that you feel slightly anxious but not overwhelmed.

Once you have your hierarchy established, choose the least intimidating item on your list as your starting point. Engage with this discomfort for a set period while employing relaxation techniques such as deep breathing or mindfulness to help manage any anxiety that arises. It's crucial to stay in this situation until your anxiety begins to decrease; this may take several minutes or longer depending on your comfort level. By repeatedly exposing yourself to this mild discomfort, you will gradually notice that it becomes less intimidating.

As you gain confidence and feel more at ease with each step, move on to the next item on your hierarchy. This progression should feel natural; if at any point you find yourself feeling overwhelmed, it's perfectly acceptable to take a step back and revisit previous levels until you feel ready to advance again. Listening to your body's signals is paramount; everyone's pace will differ based on individual experiences and comfort levels.

Throughout this process, it's important to celebrate small victories. Each time you successfully face a fear or discomfort, acknowledge your progress. This not only reinforces positive feelings but also motivates you to continue pushing through the discomfort. Remember that gradual exposure is not about eliminating anxiety entirely but rather about learning how to coexist with it without letting it dictate your actions.

Engaging in gradual exposure can also benefit from support systems—whether through friends, family, or professionals who understand the process and can provide encouragement along the way. Sharing your experiences can foster a sense of community and accountability, making the journey less isolating.

In essence, gradual exposure is about building resilience through small, manageable steps. It empowers individuals by transforming their relationship with discomfort from one of avoidance to one of acceptance and mastery. By moving at your own pace and tuning into your body's responses, you can gradually expand your comfort zone and enhance your overall quality of life.

Using Mindfulness and Self-Compassion to Cope with Difficult Emotions.

Mindfulness and self-compassion are powerful tools for navigating the emotional landscape that can arise during practices like body scans. Mindfulness is fundamentally about being present with our experiences without judgment. This means observing thoughts, feelings, and bodily sensations as they occur, allowing them to come and go without labeling them as good or bad. It invites us to engage with our emotions in a way that fosters curiosity rather than criticism. When we practice mindfulness, we cultivate an awareness that helps us recognize difficult emotions as temporary states rather than fixed aspects of ourselves. This perspective can be incredibly liberating, especially when we encounter feelings that are uncomfortable or distressing.

Self-compassion complements mindfulness beautifully. It involves treating ourselves with kindness and understanding, particularly in moments of suffering or perceived failure. Kristin Neff, a leading researcher in this field, emphasizes that self-compassion consists of three core components: self-kindness, common humanity, and mindfulness. By recognizing our shared human experience—understanding that everyone faces challenges—we can soften our inner dialogue and replace harsh self-judgment with a more nurturing voice. This shift is crucial during body scans, where we might confront feelings of inadequacy or discomfort; self-compassion allows us to acknowledge these feelings without becoming overwhelmed by them.

To cultivate mindfulness and self-compassion, several techniques can be beneficial. **Loving-kindness meditation** is one of the most well-established methods for fostering self-compassion. In this practice, individuals focus on sending positive wishes to themselves and others, repeating phrases such as, "May I be safe. May I be happy." This simple yet profound exercise not only nurtures self-kindness but also builds a sense of connection with others. When you find your mind wandering during this meditation—a natural occurrence—gently redirect your focus back to the phrases with as little judgment as possible. Each time you do this, you strengthen your ability to observe your thoughts without getting caught up in them.

Another effective technique is **journaling**, which provides a space to explore your emotions in depth. Writing about difficult experiences can help clarify feelings and reveal patterns in your emotional responses.

You might ask yourself questions like: "What am I feeling right now?" or "How can I treat myself with kindness in this moment?" Reflecting on these questions encourages a dialogue between your mindful awareness and your compassionate self.

Engaging in conversations with a trusted friend or therapist can also enhance both mindfulness and self-compassion. Sharing your experiences allows for external validation and support, which can be particularly comforting when facing challenging emotions. A compassionate listener can help you see your situation from a different perspective, reinforcing the understanding that you are not alone in your struggles.

Incorporating these practices into your daily routine fosters emotional resilience over time. Just as physical exercise strengthens the body, regular engagement with mindfulness and self-compassion techniques fortifies our mental and emotional well-being. The key is consistency; making these practices a regular part of life allows them to become ingrained habits that support us through difficult times. By nurturing both mindfulness and self-compassion, we build a solid foundation upon which we can stand firm against life's inevitable challenges.

Body Wisdom

Listening to your body's signals is an essential practice that can significantly enhance your overall well-being. In our fast-paced lives, it's easy to overlook the subtle cues our bodies send us, but these signals—whether they manifest as pain, fatigue, or restlessness—are vital indicators of our physical and emotional states. Each sensation carries a message, urging us to pay attention and respond with care. By cultivating a deeper awareness of these bodily communications, we can foster a more harmonious relationship with ourselves, leading to improved health and emotional satisfaction.

Physical sensations often serve as the body's way of expressing discomfort or imbalance. Pain, for instance, is not merely a nuisance; it is a crucial signal that something may be wrong. Fatigue can indicate that your body needs rest or that you are pushing yourself beyond your limits. Similarly, feelings of restlessness might suggest that you require movement or a change in environment. Recognizing these signals is the first step toward understanding what your body truly needs. It allows you to differentiate between various states—hunger versus emotional distress, for example—and respond appropriately.

Interpreting these signals requires practice and patience. Engaging in mindfulness techniques, such as body scanning or meditation, can enhance your ability to tune into your physical sensations without judgment. This practice involves focusing on different parts of your body and noticing any feelings of tension or relaxation that arise. By doing so, you can develop a more nuanced understanding of how your body communicates its needs. Over time, this heightened awareness can lead to better self-regulation and more effective responses to the challenges you face.

Trusting your body's wisdom is paramount. When you feel pain or discomfort, it's essential to take those feelings seriously rather than dismissing them as mere inconveniences. This might mean seeking medical attention if the pain persists or engaging in self-care practices that promote healing and relaxation. For example, if you're feeling fatigued after a long day, allowing yourself a break or indulging in restorative activities like yoga or gentle stretching can be incredibly beneficial. Conversely, if restlessness strikes during a sedentary period, consider taking a walk or engaging in some form of physical activity to release pent-up energy.

Moreover, self-care practices play a crucial role in responding to your body's signals effectively. Simple actions like staying hydrated, maintaining a balanced diet, and ensuring adequate sleep can significantly impact how well you interpret and respond to your body's needs. Additionally, nurturing emotional health through practices such as journaling or talking with friends can help you process feelings that might otherwise manifest as physical discomfort.

Listening to your body is not just about responding reactively; it's also about fostering a proactive approach to health and well-being. By developing a routine that includes regular check-ins with yourself—whether through meditation, journaling, or simply taking moments throughout the day to breathe deeply and assess how you feel—you create space for awareness and intentionality in your life. This practice empowers you to make choices that align with your physical and emotional needs.

Trusting Your Body's Innate Wisdom for Healing

The concept of the body's innate wisdom suggests that each of us possesses an inherent intelligence that guides our healing processes. This innate intelligence is not just a theoretical notion; it is a fundamental aspect of our biology, allowing us to respond to injuries and illnesses with remarkable efficiency. When we cut ourselves, for instance, our body immediately begins the process of healing by forming a clot and initiating tissue repair. This self-healing capability illustrates how the body is designed to maintain balance and restore health when given the right conditions.

Many holistic healing philosophies emphasize this innate wisdom, recognizing that our bodies have an extraordinary capacity to heal themselves. This healing process can be disrupted by stressors such as poor diet, lack of movement, or emotional turmoil, leading to discomfort or illness. However, when we create an environment that supports our body's natural processes—through proper nutrition, adequate rest, and mindfulness—we enable our innate intelligence to flourish. For example, chiropractic care operates on this principle by ensuring that the spine is aligned correctly, which facilitates optimal communication between the brain and the body. This alignment allows nerve impulses to flow freely, enhancing the body's ability to adapt and heal.

The manifestations of this innate wisdom can often be subtle yet profound. Intuition is one such example; it can guide us in making choices that align with our health and well-being. Many people experience gut feelings or "spidey senses" when something feels off in their bodies or environments. These sensations are not mere coincidences; they are signals from our body urging us to pay attention. Similarly, dreams can serve as a conduit for this wisdom, offering insights into unresolved issues or guiding us toward healing paths we may not consciously recognize.

Physical sensations also play a crucial role in communicating our body's needs. For instance, tension in specific areas may indicate emotional stress or unresolved trauma. By tuning into these sensations and acknowledging them without judgment, we can begin to understand what our bodies are trying to tell us. This awareness fosters a deeper connection with ourselves and encourages us to trust these signals as valid guides for healing.

Cultivating a relationship with our body's innate wisdom requires practice and patience. Mindfulness techniques such as meditation, breathwork, or somatic exercises can enhance our awareness of bodily sensations and emotions. By engaging in these practices regularly, we can learn to listen more attentively to our bodies and respond compassionately to their needs. This journey towards understanding and trusting our body's signals is not just about addressing physical ailments but also about embracing a holistic approach to health that honors the mind-body connection.

As we embark on this journey of self-discovery and healing, it becomes essential to remember that we are not merely passive recipients of care but active participants in our wellness journey. By nurturing this connection with our bodies and recognizing the innate wisdom within us, we empower ourselves to take charge of our health and well-being. Trusting in this process allows us to unlock the potential for true vitality and resilience that resides within each of us.

Integrating Body Wisdom into Your Daily Life

Integrating body wisdom into daily life is a transformative journey that encourages a deeper connection with oneself. To begin this process, it is essential to carve out dedicated time for self-care. This can manifest in various forms, from setting aside moments for meditation in the morning to taking leisurely walks in nature. These practices not only promote relaxation but also create space for self-reflection, allowing individuals to tune into their bodies and recognize the subtle signals they send throughout the day. Regular check-ins with oneself—perhaps every few hours—can help cultivate a habit of listening to bodily sensations and emotional states, fostering a greater awareness of how one's body feels in different contexts.

Mindfulness plays a crucial role in this integration. By practicing mindfulness, individuals can learn to be present with their thoughts, feelings, and physical sensations without judgment. This practice can be enhanced through techniques such as breathwork or guided body scans, which encourage a compassionate exploration of one's inner landscape. Engaging in regular physical activity is another vital component; whether it's yoga, dancing, or simply walking, movement helps to release pent-up emotions and invigorate the body. The rhythm of physical activity not only strengthens the body but also serves as a reminder of the joy found in movement and the importance of maintaining an active lifestyle.

Creating a daily routine that supports both physical and emotional well-being is essential for long-term success. This routine should be flexible enough to accommodate life's unpredictability while remaining consistent enough to foster growth. Individuals might consider incorporating practices such as journaling to document their feelings and experiences or establishing rituals that promote relaxation and grounding, such as evening stretches or herbal teas before bed. The key is to find what resonates personally and to approach these practices with curiosity rather than rigidity.

Consistency and patience are paramount in developing a deeper connection with the body. As individuals embark on this journey, they may encounter challenges or days when it feels difficult to stay attuned to their body's needs. It's crucial to remember that progress is not linear; some days will be easier than others. Embracing this ebb and flow allows for a more compassionate relationship with oneself. Over time, as one continues to practice these strategies, the connection between mind and body will strengthen, leading to a more balanced and fulfilling life.

CONCLUSION

Embracing Your Healing Journey

"Healing is not about becoming perfect. It's about becoming whole." - Ernest Holmes

Key Techniques and Strategies in Healing

The book discusses several key techniques and strategies essential for the healing process, including **mindfulness, breathwork,** and **grounding exercises**. Each of these techniques plays a crucial role in fostering emotional and physical well-being.

- **Mindfulness**: This practice involves being fully present in the moment, which helps individuals become aware of their thoughts and feelings without judgment. Mindfulness can reduce anxiety and promote emotional regulation, allowing individuals to process traumatic experiences more effectively. For example, the book illustrates how mindfulness meditation can help individuals observe their bodily sensations related to trauma, leading to greater insight and acceptance.

- **Breathwork:** Breathwork techniques are employed to help regulate the nervous system and release pent-up emotions. The book highlights specific breathing exercises that can calm the mind and body, such as deep diaphragmatic breathing. These exercises facilitate a sense of safety and relaxation, making it easier for individuals to confront difficult emotions.

- **Grounding Exercises**: Grounding techniques help individuals reconnect with their bodies and the present moment. The book provides examples such as standing barefoot on the ground or focusing on tactile sensations to create a sense of stability. These practices are essential for those who may feel disconnected due to trauma, as they promote a feeling of safety and presence.

Somatic Experiencing in Trauma Healing

Somatic experiencing (SE) is a pivotal approach in trauma healing, emphasizing the body's innate wisdom to release stored trauma. Developed by Dr. Peter Levine, SE focuses on bodily sensations rather than solely on thoughts or emotions associated with traumatic events. This method is particularly effective for deep-seated trauma because it addresses the physiological responses that accompany trauma, allowing individuals to process experiences without being overwhelmed by memories or emotions.

Unlike traditional talk therapies that primarily engage cognitive processes, somatic experiencing encourages clients to explore their physical sensations. This "bottom-up" approach helps individuals recognize their body's responses to stress and trauma, facilitating emotional regulation and healing. For instance, SE techniques like **titration** (gradually revisiting traumatic memories) and **pendulation** (moving between states of distress and calm) allow clients to process trauma incrementally, reducing the risk of re-traumatization.

Importance of Self-Compassion and Self-Care

Self-compassion and self-care are emphasized as vital components of the healing journey. The book underscores the necessity of setting boundaries to protect one's emotional space, which is crucial for sustained healing. Engaging in activities that bring joy—such as hobbies or relaxation techniques—fosters resilience and promotes a positive mindset.

Practicing self-compassion involves treating oneself with kindness during difficult times rather than engaging in self-criticism. This approach can significantly enhance emotional well-being by encouraging individuals to acknowledge their struggles without judgment.

Seeking Support from Others

The book highlights the importance of seeking support from others during the healing process. Whether through therapy, support groups, or trusted friends and family, community connection provides a sense of safety and validation. Sharing experiences with others who understand can alleviate feelings of isolation often associated with trauma.

Supportive relationships play a critical role in reinforcing self-worth and fostering resilience. The book illustrates how individuals who engage with supportive communities often experience enhanced healing outcomes, as these connections contribute to a greater sense of belonging and emotional stability.In summary, the integration of mindfulness, breathwork, grounding exercises, somatic experiencing, self-compassion, self-care practices, and community support forms a comprehensive framework for trauma healing that addresses both psychological and physiological aspects of recovery.

Moving Forward

Healing is a complex and nonlinear journey that requires both **consistency** and **patience**. Setbacks are an inherent part of this process, and understanding that healing takes time is crucial for fostering resilience.

The Nonlinear Nature of Healing

Healing is rarely a straight path; it often involves ups and downs. Setbacks can occur due to various factors, including stress, life changes, or emotional triggers. Recognizing these fluctuations as a natural part of the healing process allows individuals to be more compassionate toward themselves. This self-compassion is essential, as self-criticism can impede progress and lead to feelings of frustration or defeat.

The Importance of Patience

Patience with oneself is vital in the healing process. Healing takes time and effort, and expecting immediate results can lead to disappointment. For example, someone practicing mindfulness may not notice immediate changes in anxiety levels but will likely experience gradual improvements over time. This journey requires a commitment to ongoing practice and self-care.

Celebrating Small Wins

Recognizing and celebrating **small wins** can significantly enhance motivation and momentum in the healing process. Small wins are incremental achievements that contribute to overall progress. Examples include:
- Successfully completing a grounding exercise.
- Noticing a reduction in anxiety levels after practicing relaxation techniques.
- Maintaining a consistent journaling habit for emotional expression.

Celebrating these small victories fosters a sense of accomplishment, reinforcing the belief that progress is being made, even if it feels slow at times.

The Role of Consistency

Consistency plays a critical role in the healing journey. Regular practice of healing techniques—whether through therapy, exercise, or mindfulness—can lead to cumulative benefits over time. For instance:

- **Therapeutic Sessions:** Regular attendance at therapy sessions helps build a strong therapeutic relationship and allows for continuous progress tracking.

- **Physical Movement:** Consistent physical activity can strengthen the body and improve mental health by creating new neural pathways that enhance overall well-being.

To maintain consistency, consider:
- Setting a regular schedule for practice.
- Joining a supportive community or group that shares similar goals.
- Keeping track of progress to visualize improvements over time.

Self-Compassion Amid Setbacks

In moments of setback, practicing **self-compassion** is crucial. Instead of succumbing to self-criticism, individuals should remind themselves that setbacks are part of the healing process. This approach fosters resilience and perseverance, allowing one to bounce back more effectively after challenges arise. Compassionate self-talk can replace negative thoughts with affirmations that acknowledge the difficulty of the journey while reinforcing commitment to healing.

A Message of Hope, Encouragement, and Self-Compassion

As we draw this chapter to a close, let us take a moment to embrace the profound truth that healing is not only possible but also within your reach. Each of us carries within us an incredible reservoir of strength and resilience, often waiting to be tapped into. You have the power to overcome the challenges you face, and every step you take—no matter how small—brings you closer to a brighter tomorrow.

The Importance of Self-Compassion

In this journey of healing, self-compassion is your greatest ally. It is essential to treat yourself with the same kindness and understanding that you would offer a dear friend. Acknowledge your struggles without judgment, and remember that it's okay to feel vulnerable. By practicing self-compassion, you foster resilience and well-being, allowing yourself the grace to grow through adversity.

You Are Not Alone

As you navigate this path, know that you are not alone. There is a vast community of individuals who understand your pain and are rooting for your success. You are surrounded by people who care deeply about your healing process. Together, we can create a supportive network that uplifts and inspires one another.

Words of Affirmation

Take a moment to affirm your worth:
- You are enough.
- Your feelings are valid.
- Every effort you make towards healing is significant.

Let these affirmations resonate within you as reminders of your inherent value and strength.

A Call to Action

Now is the time to take the next step in your healing journey. Consider trying a new technique that resonates with you—perhaps journaling, meditation, or reaching out for support from friends or professionals. Whatever it may be, allow yourself the opportunity to explore different avenues of healing.

Above all, continue to practice self-care. Prioritize activities that nurture your mind, body, and spirit. Remember, each day is a new chance to cultivate compassion for yourself and embrace the journey ahead.

In closing, hold onto hope and trust in your capacity for growth. You are on a remarkable journey toward healing, and with each step forward, you are creating a life filled with possibility and joy. Embrace this journey with an open heart and know that brighter days are ahead.